THE TEACHING FOR SOCIAL JUSTICE SERIES

William Ayers—*Series Editor*   Therese Quinn—*Associate Series Editor*

Brave Community:
Teaching for a Post-Racist Imagination
JANINE DE NOVAIS

Humanizing Education for Immigrant and Refugee
Youth: 20 Strategies for the Classroom and Beyond
MONISHA BAJAJ, DANIEL WALSH, LESLEY BARTLETT,
& GABRIELA MARTÍNEZ

Child Care Justice: Transforming the System
of Care for Young Children
MAURICE SYKES & KYRA OSTENDORF, EDS.

Rise for Racial Justice: How to Talk About Race
With Schools and Communities
COLETTE N. CANN, KIMBERLY WILLIAMS BROWN,
& MEREDITH MADDEN

Dignity-Affirming Education: Cultivating the
Somebodiness of Students and Educators
DECOTEAU J. IRBY, CHARITY ANDERSON,
& CHARLES M. PAYNE, EDS.

Where Is the Justice? Engaged Pedagogies in
Schools and Communities
VALERIE KINLOCH, EMILY A. NEMETH,
TAMARA T. BUTLER, & GRACE D. PLAYER

Teacher Educators as Critical Storytellers:
Effective Teachers as Windows and Mirrors
ANTONIO L. ELLIS, NICHOLAS D. HARTLEP,
GLORIA LADSON-BILLINGS,
& DAVID O. STOVALL, EDS.

Surrendered: Why Progressives Are Losing the
Biggest Battles in Education
KEVIN K. KUMASHIRO

Holler If You Hear Me, Comic Edition
GREGORY MICHIE & RYAN ALEXANDER-TANNER

Same as It Never Was:
Notes on a Teacher's Return to the Classroom
GREGORY MICHIE

Spectacular Things Happen Along the Way:
Lessons from an Urban Classroom, Second Edition
BRIAN D. SCHULTZ

Teaching with Conscience in an Imperfect World:
An Invitation
WILLIAM AYERS

Worth Striking For: Why Education Policy Is Every
Teacher's Concern (Lessons from Chicago)
ISABEL NUÑEZ, GREGORY MICHIE,
& PAMELA KONKOL

Being Bad:
My Baby Brother and the School-to-Prison Pipeline
CRYSTAL T. LAURA

Fear and Learning in America: Bad Data, Good
Teachers, and the Attack on Public Education
JOHN KUHN

Deep Knowledge: Learning to Teach Science for
Understanding and Equity
DOUGLAS B. LARKIN

Bad Teacher! How Blaming Teachers
Distorts the Bigger Picture
KEVIN K. KUMASHIRO

Crossing Boundaries—
Teaching and Learning with Urban Youth
VALERIE KINLOCH

The Assault on Public Education: Confronting the
Politics of Corporate School Reform
WILLIAM H. WATKINS, ED.

Pedagogy of the Poor:
Building the Movement to End Poverty
WILLIE BAPTIST & JAN REHMANN

Grow Your Own Teachers:
Grassroots Change for Teacher Education
ELIZABETH A. SKINNER, MARIA TERESA GARRETÓN,
& BRIAN D. SCHULTZ, EDS.

Girl Time:
Literacy, Justice, and the School-to-Prison Pipeline
MAISHA T. WINN

Holler If You Hear Me: The Education of a Teacher
and His Students, Second Edition
GREGORY MICHIE

Controversies in the Classroom:
A Radical Teacher Reader
JOSEPH ENTIN, ROBERT C. ROSEN, &
LEONARD VOGT, EDS.

The Seduction of Common Sense: How the Right
Has Framed the Debate on America's Schools
KEVIN K. KUMASHIRO

Teach Freedom: Education for Liberation in the
African-American Tradition
CHARLES M. PAYNE & CAROL SILLS STRICKLAND,
ED-

D1566410

Brave Community

Teaching for a Post-Racist Imagination

Janine de Novais

Foreword by Robin D. G. Kelley

TEACHERS COLLEGE PRESS

TEACHERS COLLEGE | COLUMBIA UNIVERSITY
NEW YORK AND LONDON

Published by Teachers College Press,® 1234 Amsterdam Avenue, New York, NY 10027

Copyright © 2023 by Teachers College, Columbia University

Library of Congress Cataloging-in-Publication Data is available at loc.gov

ISBN 978-0-8077-6782-5 (paper)
ISBN 978-0-8077-6783-2 (hardcover)
ISBN 978-0-8077-8146-3 (ebook)

Printed on acid-free paper
Manufactured in the United States of America

For Jalen, who raised me just as I raised him

Contents

Foreword

I first met Janine de Novais at Columbia University in the fall of 2004. I had recently joined the faculty in African American Studies, and she worked for the Center for the Core Curriculum. Janine attended a public talk I gave on U.S. imperialism titled "We Threaten the World," and then asked to take my graduate course, "Black Revolt and the Modern World," the following spring. I rarely admit anyone to a graduate seminar who isn't enrolled in a graduate program, but I made an exception for Janine. She was smart, well-read, candid, radical, and yet never took herself too seriously. Her Ivy League education mattered less to her than being a single mother, an immigrant from Cabo Verde, a follower of her fellow countryman and revolutionary thinker Amílcar Cabral, and an activist. As an undergraduate she had participated in the 1996 protests that established Columbia's Ethnic Studies Program. She came to my class undeterred by the heavy reading load or the twenty advanced graduate students enrolled. And they were an impressive group: Two-thirds went on to hold faculty positions and publish books of their own, and the rest included a prominent actress and writer, a future maverick in the nonprofit funding world, and a brilliant abolitionist and poet who would become San Francisco's poet laureate. Needless to say, Janine not only held her own but never shied away from speaking her truth. She was brave.

Whether in her weekly journals, short essays, or classroom discussion, Janine always found a way to bring up the core curriculum, a 2-year "great books" curriculum required of all Columbia undergraduates. At the time, the administration was patting themselves on the back for adopting a few more non-white authors and inviting philosopher Anthony Appiah to speak on W. E. B. Du Bois's *The Souls of Black Folks*. But Janine wasn't interested in merely adding color to the Western canon; rather, she wanted to reorient the core altogether. She wanted more texts and context that would constitute, as she explained in her class journal, "a 'counter Core Curriculum' discourse that resides at the center—doesn't occur outside or develops somewhat extricated from the rest of this canon." She proposed a deeper reading of Du Bois's other works, the introduction of Edward Said's

Orientalism, and several landmark feminist texts dispersed across the syllabus. Her suggestion was followed by a righteous rant: "Nothing of the sort is read in Contemporary Civilization when Locke or Paine or Hume or all these guys are read. Not only is it politically reprehensible, it's also pedagogically unsound because students who wish to generate a critique . . . do not have the textual 'legitimacy' afforded others who don't have a critical view of the 'canon' *per se.*" "Modern" texts, she complained, were not introduced until the end of the second semester, as if all the anti-colonial, anti-racist, anti-foundational ideas "were never thought before all the dead white dudes were done talking, and the world as we know it had been 'made' so to speak."

Clearly, Janine had begun to plant the seeds of Brave Community praxis nearly 20 years ago. She understood then the need for students to be grounded, to see the world in its entirety and fullness, and to recognize that oppressed people are not merely victims of a racist, patriarchal, colonial system but its sharpest critics and ultimately its gravediggers. For her, changing the canon was not a project of diversity or inclusion, but one of *transformation.*

When I saw Janine again 10 years later, she was a doctoral student at Harvard's School of Education and I was giving a talk at Tufts University, a version of which was published in the *Boston Review* as "Black Study, Black Struggle." Turns out, we were both wrestling with similar issues—the relationship between pedagogy, the production of knowledge, and movements for Black liberation. But where I was exposing the university's complicity with neoliberal racism, Janine was finding ways to teach students how to understand and ultimately work toward dismantling racism. She was way ahead of me. Immersed in the research that would become the basis of *Brave Community,* Janine wanted to find out how to help students "experience that feeling where race/racism becomes a graspable, visible (at least increasingly) object in front of you, ripe for your inquiry, something you can actually get to work on understanding and dismantling" (email to me, 11/28/2015).

Brave Community is the culmination of years of research and practice. She discovered that an honest interrogation of race and racism requires a grounding in scholarly knowledge and a culture that encourages deep listening, mutual respect, and "resilient empathy." Janine argues that it is not enough to understand racism at the structural or material level. She reminds us that racism is cultural, a form of knowledge, a way of thinking and seeing that is learned and therefore must be unlearned. Invoking Cabral, she writes, "Any racial emancipation project also must be an interruption of this racist learning; it must be a critical pedagogical sparking of the imagination."

To be clear, *Brave Community* is not proposing to replace "fake news" of racism with some objective, transcendent truth; it does not fall prey to the liberal enlightenment trap of pitting "knowledge" against "ignorance." All knowledge is ideological and therefore political. In a world where power is concentrated in the hands of a few who benefit from the exploitation and suffering of others, a knowledge regime is necessary to normalize inequality to those excluded from power. Racism works to convince most exploited and oppressed white people that their interests align with the whites who actually exercise power; that one day they will become a slaveholder, boss, or a CEO, which many have come to see as entitlement rather than privilege; that there are material benefits to being white, such as higher relative wages, higher property values, greater safety and mobility, and freedom from the kinds of structural discrimination that hinder non-white people's ability to build wealth and live longer lives. Learning racism entails learning what it means to *not* be white. The spectacle of racism in practice teaches white people the consequences of being Black or Brown. Hyper-policing, premature death, caging, deportation, relegation to segregated neighborhoods and dilapidated housing, houselessness, job insecurity, and racially segmented occupations are indicators that Black and Brown lives are devalued. And yet, the devaluation of Black lives has never made the majority of white folks wealthy, healthy, or even secure. Why? Because whiteness is a deception that must always be reproduced in order to maintain class power. The 500-year-old myth of white superiority has enabled the rulers of all of us to "capture" exploited white workers as junior partners in the settler state.

Although Janine employs the term "racial ignorance," she does not use it to signify an absence of knowledge but, rather, a particular kind of distorted knowledge that is actively cultivated. For example, we frequently hear complaints that our schools "ignore" the history of slavery, Jim Crow, Indigenous dispossession, or anything having to do with marginalized people. This is not true. A radically distorted version of these histories have long occupied a place in school curricula precisely because they promote racist myths at the heart of the national narrative. Generations of students learned that white people settled the wilderness, took rightful ownership of the land from bloodthirsty Indians who didn't know what to do with it, and brought the gift of civilization and democracy not just to North America but to the rest of the world. During the first half of the 20th century at least, students were taught that "Negroes" were perfectly happy as slaves, until some conniving Republicans, carpetbaggers and such persuaded them otherwise. Leading history books by Ivy League professors repeated the myth, and D.W. Griffiths made the first epic film depicting how the great and noble Ku Klux Klan saved America from the evils of Reconstruction. Of course, these narratives were *always* contested by brave communities of scholars, an especially poignant example being W. E. B. Du Bois's epic text, *Black Reconstruction in America*, which included a final chapter calling out the ideological war on truth masquerading as objective scholarship. He aptly called that chapter, "The Propaganda of History."

If all knowledge is, indeed, ideological and therefore political, then *Brave Community* is designed to produce *insurgent knowledge*, which is to say, knowledge that refuses normalization, critiques the current arrangements, explains their origins and persistence, demands change, and offers alternatives. The Brave Community model builds on a long tradition of insurgent education, from the anti-colonial schools of the African Independence Party of Guinea and Cabo Verde (PAIGC), the Highlander Folk School in Tennessee, the citizenship schools led by Septima Clark, to the Freedom Schools launched by the Student Non-Violent Coordinating Committee and their later iteration in Detroit organized by Grace and Jimmy Boggs. In Mississippi, the Freedom Schools were intended to create "an educational experience for students which will make it possible for them to challenge the myths of our society, to perceive more clearly its realities and to find alternatives and ultimately, new directions for action."[1] Students and teachers worked together to understand power along the axes of race and class. They learned how racism benefited wealthy whites and the political class, subjugated Black people, and arrested the economic development of poor whites. And they came to the realization that their task was not to integrate an unequal society but to transform it. Similar to the Freedom schools, Brave Community is not simply about introducing new content and changing the narrative. It is a collective process that transforms our perspective and perception and builds solidarity around the goal of achieving a post-racist society.

Insurgent knowledge is always met with counterinsurgency. All of these early "brave communities" faced some level of repression and marginalization. Leaders, educators, and students in these insurgent educational spaces were subject to surveillance, charged with sedition, harassed, fired from their jobs, and sometimes subject to violence. Besides, the status quo upholds its national myths by silencing its critics, labeling them communists, troublemakers, quacks, unqualified, and dangerous. When the late historian William Loren Katz began teaching and writing about race in the late 1950s, he recalled, "[I]t seemed un-American to depict the evils of slavery and disloyal to talk about African-American people fighting for freedom against whites. Omitting, neglecting, or suppressing the facts of slave defiance became a lasting American tradition."[2] In 1961, the Meriden, Connecticut, chapter of the Daughters of the American Revolution organized a successful campaign to remove all "subversive" textbooks from schools and libraries. The ban included any books that contained images of poverty, material on the United Nations, prejudice, mental health, and the writings of "liberal, racial, socialist, or labor agitators."[3]

Today such attacks are all too familiar. Since Donald Trump's election, the Right has invoked "Critical Race Theory" as a code for any acknowledgment of racism, sexism, or related forms of oppression and subjugation occurring in the United States. They have launched a campaign using the law and bullying tactics to declare war on "critical race theory" (CRT)—banning books and curricula dealing with racism, sexism, or gender identity.[4] McCarthyism has returned. A group called "Moms for Liberty" in New Hampshire offered a $500 bounty for turning in teachers who violate the state's anti-CRT law. In April 2022, Florida Governor Ron DeSantis signed into law the "Stop Wrongs to Our Kids and Employees Act," or Stop WOKE Act, which prohibits teaching anything that can be interpreted as causing "guilt, anguish, or other forms of psychological distress" in students for any harms done by "other members of the same race, color, sex, or national origin." Iowa Governor Kim Reynolds signed a similar bill that criminalizes teaching content deemed "divisive" by the state, including subject matter that might make "any individual . . . feel discomfort, guilt, anguish, or any other form of psychological distress on account of that individual's race or sex."[5]

Absurd and illogical as these laws are, the current war on CRT and "wokeness" are not the handiwork of hicks. The campaign is carefully contrived propaganda based not on winning the argument but the suppression of any critique of racism, patriarchy, trans- and homophobia. But conservatives and white nationalists are not the only obstacle to a just, post-racist world. The work of Brave Community inevitably must come to terms with an even bigger obstacle to transformative change: liberalism. In 2022, it is easy to condemn racist extremists, egregious acts of terror, even police violence so long as they are treated as aberrations, "bad apples" in need of anti-bias training, or occasional moral lapses that deviate from our inexorable path on the road of democracy and freedom. Liberalism, which is the ideology of the status quo, promotes the myth that in the U.S. democracy is a creed passed down to us by the framers or "founding fathers" of our constitutional republic. According to this logic, racism is a moral problem that arises when the democratic, egalitarian values of the American creed conflict with the treatment of people of color. Racism can be corrected by the fair application of the rule of law. Compelling as it might seem, this national myth obscures how racism was built into the very fabric of American society—in settler colonialism, racial capitalism, patriarchy, not to mention the Constitution itself.

In this topsy-turvy world where merely calling out racism is considered racist, the need for insurgent knowledge becomes more urgent. *Brave*

Community could not be timelier. Janine de Novais has given us the model we need to free us from our comfort zones, confront difficult truths, expose the paper-thin foundations, lies, and distortions upon which racism is built, and cultivate a post-racist imagination. Most importantly, it fosters the growth of a dedicated anti-racist community, an assembly of heretics willing to challenge deeply entrenched racialized knowledge and act. What choice do we have but to be brave?

—Robin D. G. Kelley
Los Angeles, December 4, 2022

NOTES FOR FOREWORD

1. "Memorandum to Freedom School Teachers," http://www.educationand democracy.org/FSCfiles/B_08_MemoToFSTeachers.htm
2. William Loren Katz, *Breaking the Chains: African American Slave Resistance* (New York: Simon Pulse, 1998).
3. Gary B. Nash, Charlotte Crabtree, and Ross Dunn, *History on Trial: Culture Wars and the Teaching of the Past* (New York: Knopf, 1997), 69.
4. Critical Race Theory is actually a 4-decades-old body of legal scholarship that examines how structural racism persists after the introduction of anti-discrimination laws, and the ways in which the remedy to address racism can further entrench structural inequality. See Kimberlé Crenshaw, Neil Gotanda, Gary Peller, and Kendall Thomas, eds. *Critical Race Theory: The Key Writings that Formed the Movement* (New York: The New Press, 1996).
5. Jaclyn Peiser, "N.H. governor slams conservative group's $500 reward for reporting critical race teachings: 'Wholly inappropriate,'" *Washington Post*, November 19, 2021; Wallace Hettle, "Keep History Teachers Free to Teach, in Iowa and the Nation," *History News Network* (June 20, 2021), https://historynewsnetwork .org/article/180574. In August 2022, a federal judge declared the law violates the First Amendment, but the ruling does not apply to public schools or colleges, where it is still in effect. Tim Craig, "Judge blocks Florida from enforcing 'Stop Woke Act' on private companies," *Washington Post*, August 18, 2022, https:// www.washingtonpost.com/nation/2022/08/18/florida-stop-woke-act/

Acknowledgments

I am forever indebted to two outstanding teachers and their students who allowed me to accompany their learning journeys as I conducted a study of their experiences over the course of 2 years. They were vulnerable, honest, and exceedingly generous with me. Professors Thomas and Stone and their students changed my life.

Thank you, Bill Ayers and Therese Quinn, for the honor of being part of your *Teaching for Social Justice* series. Thank you to Sarah Biondello, Emily Spangler, and the entire Teachers College Press team for their support.

Sharon Lynn Bear, if you did not edit my words with such care and respect, I might never have believed that they could be shared with the world. Thank you.

Thank you, Katelyn Knox and Allison Van Deventer, for helping me shape my ideas into this book. Jake Fay, thank you for being the original *Brave Community* book whisperer. Eve L. Ewing, thank you for shining in a way that lights the way for the rest of us. Thank you to Stephany Cuevas, Nicole Deterding, Rosalie Rolón-Dow, and Elizabeth Soslau for contributing your brilliance to this book. Nadine and Jacquie Mattis, I am grateful for the wholehearted abundance of your Easton's Nook community.

My deepest gratitude goes to adrienne maree brown, without whose love and support neither this book nor I would be here. Thank you, neighbor.

To my family and friends-who-are-family, I am blessed that you are too numerous to name, that you span four generations and multiple continents, and that you love me in many languages. I could never have the right words, so I hope that my life honors you every day.

To my mother, Xanda, who is the best teacher I know, thank you for showing me that learning is a superpower. To Mama Nica and Papa Xande, a deep bow of love and gratitude for my life. To my father, Tidô, thank you for always believing. To Vovô Tê and Vó Mila, thank you for keeping watch then and now.

May all beings be safe, be happy, be healthy, and live with ease.

Brave Community

Introduction

To educate as the practice of freedom is a way of teaching that anyone can learn.

—bell hooks, *Teaching to Transgress* (2014)

We are in a struggle against those who seek to recruit people to the cause of White supremacy. In this struggle, we need tools for creating a deep and shared understanding of the relationship between racial justice and democracy. This book is one such tool. It introduces Brave Community, a method for teaching and thinking about racism that cultivates people's post-racist imagination. The post-racist imagination is the ability to think through and beyond racism. A post-racist imagination is possible even while structural racism persists. Such an ability must be learned and practiced by anyone who wants to combat racism, and Brave Community is that practice. The method leverages what I call *grounding for learning* to develop the intellectual bravery and empathy that people need to learn about racism, understand it rigorously, and know how to intervene when it occurs. Grounding for learning is a combination of content and culture. Here, content refers to *what we learn*—all the materials that provide us with evidence and data. Culture refers to *how we approach that learning and each other*, for example, ways of engaging in discussion, or sitting with a measure of discomfort that comes with encountering new information. As you can imagine, being grounded in this way is ideal in all situations in which we want to learn deeply. In any such situation, it is ideal to have content to learn and a productive culture in which to learn. In the case of learning about racism, however, this grounding is indispensable.

We need to be grounded to learn about racism because our default is ignorance. The United States thrives on a cultivation of ignorance of racism. We see it in the triumphalist narrative of its founding; what children are taught in schools erases the violent genocide of Native peoples and the colonial occupation of their lands. We see it in the perverse exceptionalism of the American story that erases the violent enslavement of Africans and the structural racism that built and sustains this society.

1

This cultivated ignorance is more than merely the absence of knowledge; it is a perversion of knowledge. The problem is not just that people do not know how racism constructs their lives. The problem is that people are pumped full of lies. Our educational system and wider culture profess that the supremacy of White people is real, that racists are only a minority of White people who are amoral monsters, and that racism is an inevitability instead of a practice invented to justify the unjustifiable: genocide, enslavement, and colonization of fellow humans in the service of greed.

Widespread racial segregation worsens this cultivated ignorance. By and large, people do not experience intimacy or conviviality with people who are racially different. We do not learn the reality of multiracial democracy in schools and universities or experience it in our lives. What people of color do not know about how racism functions harms our ability to become free of it, compounding the already powerful forces that work against us. What White people do not know about racism harms their ability to become free of it because it shelters them from the accountable reckoning that they must do. Ultimately, this cultivated ignorance recruits us all to support a racist status quo that demeans us and that we abhor. I am aware that some people will not see themselves in this "we" that I invoke. That is okay. I am not addressing them. I am addressing the people who feel called to the promise of democracy.

We are stuck because we cannot imagine a world beyond racism. We are stuck because, let's face it, engaging with issues of racism in mixed company produces immense acrimony and little result. We're over it, we're tired, someone else can try it.

I developed Brave Community over almost a decade of research and teaching precisely to address this challenge. The approach is singularly focused on creating ideal conditions to replace the defensiveness that we usually bring to this issue with the kind of empowerment that can come only from learning. Brave Community works because teaching and learning work. In this book, I will show you exactly how to use this method, by integrating what I learned through research, my own practice, and the people who shared learning spaces with me.

FROM RESEARCH TO PRACTICE: A BRIEF OVERVIEW

Before Brave Community was a method, it was a theory that I developed over a 2-year period. I studied two college classrooms at a private, elite institution that I will call "Gable University."[1] Gable is a predominantly White institution. At the time I conducted my study (2014–2015), 90% of its faculty and senior administrators were White, as was half of its undergraduate student body. A fifth of those students were international.

Less than 1% of the undergraduate students identified as Native, 5% as Black, 10% as Latinx, and 15% as Asian. My study explored the relationship between classroom experience and students' understanding of race (de Novais, 2021).

A large body of research demonstrates that racial diversity and engagement with race-related content makes students smarter and better prepared for life in our diverse democracy: Learning about and in the presence of racial diversity increases our ability to think critically, helps us to interact better with people who are racially different during and after our educational experiences, and raises our awareness and understanding of racism. Although I am most familiar with research situated in higher education and K–12 education settings, there are studies about the benefits of racial diversity for nearly every sector of society.[2] Although this research on the benefits to students of learning about racial and cultural diversity is well established, not much is known about how to ensure that learning is productive.

Given the never-ending racial strife in society at large, I wanted to understand what professors did to be successful in the difficult but urgent work of teaching about race and racism. I spent a few months contacting professors who taught courses that addressed issues related to race and racism, were highly rated by students on evaluations, and were at universities near me. Unlike K–12 teachers who are often observed while teaching, most college professors I asked did not want to be observed in the intimate space of their classrooms. In the end, only two professors allowed me to propose my study to their students. When people are curious about why I ended up studying two male professors, my speculative answer is, first, that they were the ones who would allow me, and second, that perhaps their gender, as well as experience, contributed to their confidence.

During the fall, my focus was Professor Charles Thomas's course, Writing Slavery. It was a 22-student seminar in African American literature, focused on narratives written by people who were enslaved. The following semester, I sat in on Professor Isaac Stone's "Liberation and Race Politics" course. This course was, in contrast, a weekly lecture for about 60 students, complemented by smaller, weekly discussion sections of about 10 students. I attended all class sessions and took notes about everything that happened during class—not just what was said but also how it was said, the body language of the speaker, and that of listeners. I noted when there was lively discussion and when the tensions slowed them down. I noted silences and thought about their motives being as varied as the number of students. To make sure that I could follow along, as well as be an informed interviewer, I read all the course materials. I interviewed the professors only once each semester—a rookie mistake I still regret. I interviewed each student three times: at the start of the course, at the end, and once more, about 6 months or so afterward.

When I started my study in fall of 2014, many college students arrived on campus reeling from the horrific image of 18-year-old Michael Brown, lying on the street in his neighborhood in Ferguson, MO, after being shot to death by the police. Brown should have started college that September as well. Just a month earlier, in July, Eric Garner was choked to death by a New York City police officer. These two murders reenergized the Black Lives Matter protests that had first erupted when the killer of Trayvon Martin was acquitted 2 years before. By the following year, Baltimore had risen up to protest the killing of Freddie Gray. These brutal realities shaped the classroom experiences that the professors and students allowed me to observe.

After my study, I took about a year to analyze all the data and understand what answers, what story of learning, they offered me. What I found came in waves. Most salient at first was the bravery that students displayed over the course of the class. It was not, they told me in interviews, what they usually experienced. They, like most of us, were used to anticipating and experiencing superficiality or tension in discussions of racism. They were surprised to find themselves able to push beyond their comfort zone and toward intellectual risks.

Then, probing more into what they told me and what I had observed, I determined that the professors had established conditions that made that bravery possible: They had set the stage, in their own distinct ways, for students to ask hard questions, move through uncomfortable topics, and change their minds. Finally, I understood that each student's brave comment was bravely listened to by their colleagues. Each student's attempt at changing and growing their ideas was received by their professor and their peers with trust and spaciousness. In both courses, people gave one another room to learn. Putting it all together, I concluded first that, because the students were grounded for learning, they developed more intellectual bravery and empathy. I called that process Brave Community. Second, I observed that being able to learn about racism in an environment that promoted being brave and empathetic helped the students to develop a deeper, more empowered understanding of racism—something I call the *post-racist imagination.*

By the end of my study at Gable, the Black Lives Matter (BLM) movement was also inspiring activism in schools and campuses across the United States. Students took inspiration from BLM to demand the end of White supremacist practices at their schools and colleges. Teachers and administrators in higher education and K–12 settings alike were asking for guidance on how to approach these topics with learners. (I am speaking about 2015, and it pains me to know that I could be speaking of 2020, or 2022.) The intervening years also marked my transition from graduate student to newly minted professor. In other words, I went from studying professors who taught about racism to becoming one myself. It was for these reasons that I was inspired to translate my study findings into a useful method that I could use in my own classrooms, teach to other practitioners across the educational and cultural sectors, and now teach to you, reader.

IMAGINING THAT THE IMPOSSIBLE IS POSSIBLE

Racism is only five hundred and some odd years old. Most of us think that the category of race is older than it actually is. In fact, historians trace the emergence of racism to the inception of the transatlantic slave trade (Desmond & Emirbayer, 2009, 2016; Fields & Fields, 2022). Intergroup strife, various forms of oppression, and prejudice based on regional or cultural difference, even slavery, have existed since antiquity, but *race and racism* are not that old. The concept of race we have today emerged as a justification for the enslavement of African people (Painter, 2010). During those centuries, history shows us that racism has always been contested and rejected by most of the people who are not positioned atop a racial hierarchy. Even though racism has not always been there, it feels like it has. That is why James Baldwin (2013) famously referred to ending racism as "the impossible," in *The Fire Next Time.* Crucially, Baldwin demanded that we pursue this impossibility because we had achieved it before:

> I know that what I am asking is impossible. But in our time, as in every time, the impossible is the least that one can demand—and one is, after all, emboldened by the spectacle of human history in general, and American Negro history in particular, for it testifies to nothing less than the perpetual achievement of the impossible. (p. 104)

As a product of that "perpetual achievement of the impossible," I have always experienced the power of understanding how the world works. I have always known that the point of learning is to be free. The point of reading, of listening to my grandparents, my parents, and my teachers, was to cultivate the skills to achieve my freedom. In retrospect, I realize that this was because I understood that my freedom could be taken from me. Ours was freedom that had been taken before, from many people like us, across the expanse of place and time. When the modern world first became the monument to unfreedom that it is today, all its maps and codes and ways of knowing served the project of Black enslavement. Black people had to learn how to find freedom inside of its absence—a feat of the imagination. My freedom was imagined, dreamed up, and talked and read about before it could be won. The people who did that work on my and everyone's behalf were freedom learners as much as they were freedom fighters.

I was born in 1976, just one year after the independence of my native Cabo Verde from centuries of Portuguese rule. I was born free under the flag of the P.A.I.C.G. (the *Partido Africano para Independencia de Guiné e Cabo Verde*), the flag that inspires this book's cover. This was the political party that Amílcar Cabral and others founded in the fight for independence. It would be years until, while studying in New York City, I understood Cabral's standing as one of the greatest philosophers of Black liberation in world history.

As a child, he was my personal hero and my idea of freedom made flesh. I learned that Cabral and his comrades found their political vision while in college. As the nerdy kid that I was, it was thrilling to learn that nerds could become revolutionaries. The revolutionary songs that I learned, such as "Flor de nos Revolução" by Dani Mariano and the band Kings, were about our inheritance as children of a newly freed nation:

> First Cabral told us, the children are the flower of our revolution. Then Cabral showed us, they are the fruits of tomorrow. Children of Cabo Verde, study and progress, for the future of the country. Pick up your books, pick up your pen . . . (Kings, 1973)

This focus on learning made sense to me. Cabral (1974) said:

> Just as happens with the flower in a plant, in culture there lies the capacity (or the responsibility) for forming and fertilizing the seedling which will assure the continuity of history, at the same time assuring the prospects for evolution and progress of the society in question. (p. 13)

He means, in part, that the future blooms from our cultivation of the present conditions; that is, freedom must be tended through culture or everyday practice.

Because I have been Black in different contexts, I know that racism is not merely a structural project but also a cultural one. I know that a racist society teaches racism to all its people every day to sustain itself. I know that racism is learned, and, as such, it can be unlearned. Further, as Cabral taught us, the cultivation of that unlearning is as crucial as any aspect of the struggle. Any racial emancipation project also must be an interruption of this racist learning; it must be a critical pedagogical sparking of the imagination.

Using the Brave Community method will not inoculate you against the complications that arise when you teach, learn, or think together about racism in a racist society. Rather, by using the method, you and your learners, colleagues, and community will have a better chance to resolve these complications in a way that serves the learning and serves you. Let me also say that using the Brave Community method will not suffice to dismantle racism. Nevertheless, here is what I can say to you unequivocally: It would have made a tremendous difference in my son's life if even 10% of his educators had been less captive to racist thinking. If even 10% had been able to see my child as more than some Black boy trope, his life would have been markedly better between kindergarten and 12th grade. Yes, there were individual White people who were racist, but, more importantly, there was an educational system built on racist logics of Black underachievement that no one interrupted. There was, and there is still, an entire society that is unschooled and unpracticed in imagining a world beyond racist ideology. Sparking the post-racist imagination of all the teachers whose conditioning made them see my son Jalen's self-possession as confrontation, and his introversion as lack of interest, would have spared him from a world of hurt, even while structural racism persisted.

To behave as though a poison so great as racism infects only its "beneficiaries," White people, is dishonest. So is behaving as if only ultimate solutions are worth pursuing and achieving. Pretending that material solutions alone, or policies alone, will deliver us is short-sighted. We will not solve the structural problem of racism without solving the cultural problem of racist ideology. The Brave Community method is about building our capacity to do that, by teaching us to interrupt racist sense-making in everyday life. That capacity, which must be learned and practiced, is what I call the post-racist imagination. As Robin D. G. Kelley (2022) reminds us: "Without new visions, we don't know what to build, only what to tear down" (p. xii). Kelley demonstrates, in *Freedom Dreams,* that a unifying theme of Black struggles for liberation is the imagination that Black freedom, and the end of racism, are possible. Post-racism is my freedom dream, and Brave Community is the method for teaching us how to keep dreaming.

We exist between the apocalyptic arrival of strangers to foreign shores to commit unspeakable crimes against those that dwelled there and a yet unrealized future in which we suture the deep tear in the fabric of human culture that is racism. Since the racist die has been cast, none has seen a future in which people who are not White do not fear for the lives of their children. This reality is plain, and it is terrifying. I write this book because I have heard, over the years, that the Brave Community method leaves people feeling more equipped and less afraid. I write this book because I want you to feel more equipped and less afraid.

A NOTE ON WORKING WITH RACE, THE MASTER'S RUSTIEST TOOL

Ever since I first read Audre Lorde's (1984) admonishment that the master's tools will never dismantle the master's house, I have imagined race to be the most rusty, jagged, and dangerous of those tools. Handling such a tool always leaves a residue and accidental cuts to the fabric of who we are. Often, all that rust can cause an infection. And yet, we must do our work.

Race is a social construct. Put in simple terms, it was invented as a category for sorting people to advantage people said to be White at the expense of people said to be not White. In the early stages of the formation of slaveholding settler colonial societies, such as the United States, this invented category called "race" became necessary to justify the systematic and violent abuse of Indigenous and African people. The invented racist logic works like this: Some people can be savagely and perpetually abused, exploited, removed, or exterminated because they are, in fact, Not People. Hundreds of brutal years later, this fable has become so politically and culturally real that many mistake it for natural and permanent. It is neither. For this reason, when we contemplate discussing race, we face a dilemma. On the one hand, we must talk and think about it to stay vigilant, because racism is adaptive and productive; it never rests, so we can never rest. On the other hand, talking about race both conjures it and increases its power. Like a spell, talking of race always risks recasting its domination over us. The imperfect way that I resolve this dilemma is twofold. One, I make my thinking on it transparent, as I just did. Two, I carefully choose when (and determine why) race does or does not matter to my thinking.

WHEN RACE MATTERS

Although I appreciate that capitalizing words such as Black, White, or Indigenous makes race appear more real, I do it. Today, much more than the original racist fable from the 1500s resides in those words. I capitalize those words because, for me, they are proper nouns, like Cabo Verdean, that designate a particular, meaningful category of experience. As Imani Perry (2022) stated so succinctly in discussing why she does the same:

> I do so because the categories, Black and White, were made together. They are strangely symbiotic, opposing yet intimate. . . . These are identity categories that were made by law, custom, policies, protest, economic relations and, perhaps most potently, culture. Politeness, grammar rules, and political pieties aside, this strikes me as a simple truth that ought to be acknowledged. I didn't make the rules. I am trying to tell them to you. (xi)

WHEN RACE DOESN'T MATTER

Let me tell you about a rule that I *did* make and explain my reasoning: The Brave Community method is the same, regardless of who you are. The method recognizes only two categories of people: teachers and learners. Every person, irrespective of their identity, can be a teacher-learner, capable and deserving of an education that sets that person free. In these pages and in Brave Community practice, sorting people based on race is neither practical nor ethical. Practically speaking, I could never properly anticipate how any one person would experience the Brave Community method based on their race. What we may know, in the aggregate, about a group of people identified racially is not at all determinant of how any individual human being experiences their learning. Ethically speaking, critical pedagogy is liberatory, and people's liberation far exceeds the narrow cast of their socially ascribed identities. The whole point of learning is to change who we are, to end up somewhere other than where we began, to evolve. If I tried to predict anyone's journey based on their identity, I would be taking something from them. For this reason, Brave Community is a theory that refuses to reify—or overly emphasize—racial identity; instead, it concerns itself with how all learners are similarly capable of intellectual bravery and empathic resilience. This means that, on these pages, I will reference the race of people minimally. I do this to invite you to practice discovering something beyond our handed-down ideas about race.

CHAPTER 1

Grounding for Learning

THE POWER OF THE CLASSROOM

You're Black so you need to excel in class because people are going to try to hold you back. And so, I just wasn't raised to seek comfort; I was raised to be excellent. I think, be confident. I don't really think about being comfortable.

—Jessica, student

When Jessica answered my question about her level of comfort in the classroom, I felt as if I knew her, even though I had just met her. Jessica was one of the first students in Professor Thomas's class who agreed to be interviewed. As someone who was also raised to be excellent at all costs, I recognized in her words the armor that shields from vulnerability. When you are raised as Jessica was, you understand that the world is hostile to you and that your excellence must be more than an achievement; it must be a protection. Expecting to overcome that hostility through excellence is a preemptive strike of Black students against the great many "weapons formed against" their minds and hearts.

"So, I've been doing a word association thing with everyone at the start of the interview," I told her next. I sounded like I didn't know what I was really doing because, well, I didn't. This was my first time conducting a research study. Jessica seemed to warm up immediately to my nerdy nervousness.

"Okay, sounds great!" she said, exceedingly warmly, to reassure me.

"If I say, 'discussing race in the classroom,' what's the first word that comes to mind?" I asked.

Jessica took time to think. She began to formulate her thoughts, first through sounds and facial expressions: a sigh, some raised eyebrows, then a half smirk, then another sigh.

"I think," she started, her eyes apparently scrolling through the few options in her head, "I'm going to say *hesitation*." I asked her to elaborate.

I think, in class, I'm often very vocal. But I always find myself having a bit of pause in a class that discusses race in a way that I just don't in other subjects because I think I'm more conscious about, "Am I saying the right thing, how am I phrasing this," if I'm pushing back against another kid especially, a kid who's not Black. I know that my personality can be intimidating, and I'm called an angry Black woman all the time. I just find myself sort of going through these mental checks and filters in my head more.

Schools and, later, universities socialize their students, as that is their function. Unfortunately, only a minority of students finds this to be a pleasant experience. These lucky few tend to be some combination of White, middle or upper class, cisgendered, heterosexual, ablebodied, neurotypical, and born in the United States or of U.S. parents. These atypical students feel seen, understood, and allowed to be themselves in educational spaces. Most students do not experience that; they experience school as a constraint on their personalities.

There is, however, a particular experience of hostility that students of color face. Centuries of White supremacist mythology about our inferiority "in the endowments both of body and mind" have made us illegitimate intellectuals (Jefferson, 1785). We enter school knowing that we are considered less smart, less capable, less deserving of respect. In college, we are seen as undeserving recipients of affirmative action. To this considerable burden is added the challenge of discussing racism in classrooms.

Time and time again, the students of color I interviewed answered my word association prompt with similar words: apprehension, awkwardness, tension. This was not surprising. What was surprising, however, was how similar the answers from White students were. There is an optimal level of challenge where learning occurs, but in this situation, the students were speaking of situations in which the classroom atmosphere made learning difficult.

Despite what the students told me, over the course of Thomas's class, they did not have negative or uncomfortable experiences. They warmed up to one another, to the material, and to Thomas right away, and off they went. Their discussions, despite the difficulty of the topic, were deep and fearless. This fearlessness surprised them. As Lyor expressed, they were pleasantly surprised:

The thing that I hate about most of the classes here is that everybody is just so kind of complacent. Even the language that we use to disagree with people is super light. You don't disagree, you "push back" or you "play Devil's advocate" as a way of kind of avoiding any accountability, you know? But in this class, people are actively disagreeing, even intensely. That's probably my favorite part. It feels like an interactive, dynamic class, where you're building on things others are saying.

Over the course of the semester, I saw what this honesty and accountability allowed students to learn. In Thomas's class, one of the most robust, semester-long discussions drew on historian Barbara J. Fields's article, "Slavery, Race and Ideology in the United States of America"(Fields & Fields, 2014). In this widely influential article, Fields explains that the historical archive clearly shows that racism was deployed to justify and sustain the economic system of slavery—not the other way around. In the final class of the semester, Thomas posed a question to his students that allowed new information to reshape their thinking:

> Fields argues that race is a fraudulent fiction in a way, tied to its historical context. It is psychologically and culturally unstable and yet its power is like nothing else in the history of the world. So are we perpetuating it by discussing it, without considering that, as Fields says?

Kevin said that he was "impatient" with what he saw as Fields's "oversimplification": "No! Because how is [race] eradicable now? How could we just stop talking about it? I don't buy that we can eradicate it that simply, the differences among us, that stuff matters, those things are real."

Lyor added nuance: "Saying something is real does not mean it's not created or constructed. Just because it's socially created doesn't mean it's not real."

Jessica and Deyanira exchanged smiles, which usually meant that they were about to interject, which Deyanira did:

> Fields is saying we're not talking about it in *the right way*. Yeah, we wrestle with that essay because it's really complicated. I think Fields is saying since it was made once, since it was done, race can be undone.

As I observed the students responding to this statement, I recognized that they were exploring the possibility that something could be done to change aspects of the racial status of their own lives. Racism, something that felt intractable in their own minds, began to feel malleable because they understood it better.

The following semester, Stone's students had similar experiences. They were willing to reconsider long-held points of view in light of what they were learning. An issue that was foremost on students' minds was the role of White people who supported the Black Lives Matter protests, nationally and on their campus. In our final interview, Kenneth reflected on how his perspective on this issue had shifted after Stone's class.

> I guess, based on the class, I am more aware of conversations about the role of people who aren't Black within race relations. What space should White people have? How much solidarity should we have? It makes me a little bit conflicted about the frustration some Black people have with educating people who are White. Even though no one educated me, I learned by being around people who are Black like me. These people who are White on campus may never be around people who are Black, so they definitely don't know. How are they supposed to be educated? It seems, from what I have seen [in the class], is that the loss of nuance is, like, a recent thing. You saw White people in civil rights movement marching. Even Malcolm X would go on national television to educate White people, like, "get it together, White people." Now I feel like maybe my generation has no nuance at all.

When I interviewed students from both courses for the final time, I revisited the word association question: In our first interview, I asked what word discussing race in the classroom makes you think of. How would you answer that question today?

Whereas earlier, the words had been variations of discomfort and disappointment, now students said words such as "empowering," "fundamental," and "life-changing." They mentioned that understanding the history of racism made them feel "equipped" for the world. Keli'i told me that it made him feel like he could translate, or "bridge the gap," between what he had learned and his community: "So we can talk about these things in class, then go to a community rally, and then act like a messenger or translator of these important ideas."

Adina discussed the connection between learning and the lack of fear that she felt in Thomas's class:

> We are allowed to push ourselves, to take risks and ask questions. Class has these tensions, always does. But I enjoy it because that is how I learn. If you feel scared to say what you think, you don't get the same impact. Just being able to say it is a learning process in itself.

Jessica, who had gone in full of hesitation and expecting things to go badly, picked a word that grabbed me.

> I think I would say brave. I think a lot of risks were taken. I think, at the beginning of class, I was very critical. I came in with this sort of

critical eye, like, who's going to say something crazy? And I think a lot of the tension was coming from people not knowing what to say and what not to say and feeling scared to say the wrong thing. And I think, throughout the class, we sort of landed on this feeling that there isn't a wrong thing to say because a lot of us said things we wouldn't have said in other spaces. And I think that's what I'm most proud of.

BACK TO THE FIRST DAY OF CLASS

By the end of my year observing classes at Gable, I knew that learners who had expected to be scared had instead found themselves being brave in their learning about racism. My next step as a researcher was to determine *what* had helped students to exceed their own expectations. Why did both courses, taught by two very different professors, consistently and pleasantly surprise students who had expected to experience tension and apprehension? Looking at one particular final interview question pointed me back to the first week of classes. "If you had to share the recipe for what made this class work for you, what would you say?" In answering this question, students mentioned the content of the class, the culture of the class, or both. The words the students used also consistently involved the idea of a foundation. When Kenneth described how he felt, he cradled the air to depict a "lifting."

> I think the text opens people up. So, it gives you a lifting, like a place to start from, whereas if you have a random conversation with no context, there's just so many aspects [from which] you could talk about race productively. I feel like a text can kind of contextualize and say [we're looking at] this aspect. It gives you somewhere to go.

They also felt that the power of the classroom first resided with the professor. The professor had set the conditions from day one. Will, one of Stone's students, put it this way:

> I think the class, the historical and textual stuff, gives people a way to engage without endangering their politics, maybe? I think a cool thing about the class is that it provides some sort of concrete basis for people to have discussions that maybe change their minds rather than just kind of presenting ideologies. No one is persuaded by that, usually. But maybe they can be persuaded by thinking about it on their own terms.

Students also talked about how they could explore ideas without "endangering" themselves due to the culture that the professors had established. Isabelle spoke of Stone's course in this way:

> I feel like there are some commitments that you come [with] to a topic like racism that I feel can really inhibit you intellectually. And I think Prof. Stone has been really amazing at not doing that and really making this about the material, all the different approaches you can take to the subject matter. There's been no proselytizing. In some ways he really teaches you to abstract out of real life so you can think. Maybe some people think there are problems with that, but that is what I want from a classroom environment.

Warner noted how Thomas had also created an empowering environment for students:

> When I was in his class though, I didn't realize how much he was guiding that. Because his style felt more like, let me lay it all out on the table and now you go, you talk, you figure it out. So he wasn't heavy handed ever. I'm actually not sure how he did it.

From here, I went back to my analysis of the fieldnotes from each respective first day of class to figure out how both professors had "done it," how they had given students this sense of being on solid ground to learn about a difficult topic, such as racism.

Professor Charles Thomas, Fall, First Day

It is the start of the Fall semester. Today is the introductory class for Writing Slavery, a course where students read writings by and about enslaved people, to "view history through their eyes and not the eyes of their masters." Professor Charles Thomas stands in the middle of the classroom. He is an imposing but welcoming presence, with a voice that is equal parts rasp and warmth. Students expecting the boring review of course goals that often happens on the first day are pleasantly surprised. Without even glancing at the syllabus in his hand, Thomas launches into a personal story that begins with his undergraduate education at Gable. "This was, of course, ages ago," he jokes. As Thomas recounts, he wanted to write his thesis on the early African American novel, but this plan had to be approved by a very intimidating faculty member. Thomas paints a vivid picture of this fateful meeting. On one side, he positions the authoritative professor, "a towering figure in the English department," sitting in a large leather armchair in his study, a displeased look on his face. "He actually was in a tweed jacket."

Students laugh, engrossed. Thomas describes his younger self, standing on the other side, intimidated but eager to pitch his thesis idea to the skeptical professor. "I told him I wanted to write about the early Black novel and focus on writing that Black people did before emancipation. I thought it was a brilliant idea! Unfortunately, he didn't agree with my enthusiasm at all." Thomas dramatically quotes the professor's verdict to him, mimicking his disdainful tone: "Are you arguing that Black people were doing writing worthy of our attention before emancipation?" Without breaking the narrative flow, Thomas then segues into the motivation for the course he is introducing to students today: "In a very real way, I created this course because, basically, I wish I had a course like this back then, back when I was standing where you are standing. If I had a course like this, I would have known how to argue with that professor about my thesis idea." As Thomas moves through these seemingly off-the-cuff remarks that, I recognize, are planned, I admire how effortlessly he inserts his biographical details. "As a working-class Italian kid from Philly," he begins one sentence. When Thomas finally does bring up class expectations, they are fully embedded in his larger narrative. "In class, I will want you to take risks, be critical, push back, not be intellectually safe, be provocative. But respect for one another is paramount. It is important because, among other things this course is about, it is about the disrespect that the authors we will read suffered, as Black people. The least we can do is have enough respect for their texts and for one another. We must model the kind of respect that wasn't present in the lives of the people we will read."

Professor Isaac Stone, Spring, First Day

One semester later. I'm at the first meeting of Black Liberation Politics, Professor Isaac Stone's course. I look around at what is, in many ways, a classic classroom, located in one of the oldest lecture halls of the main campus. The classroom has that mix of dark wood paneling, high ceiling, and giant windows that Hollywood studios favor when filming college scenes. The classroom doesn't feel imposing. It just feels dignified, like Isaac Stone himself, when he walks up to the front of the room in a dark brown three-piece suit. In this lecture hall, the professor stands on a stage, about three feet above floor level. Stone dives right in and lays out his motivations for teaching the course by explaining the ongoing frustration that he felt with having the material isolated in a specific "Black" course. "These thinkers are crucially important to modern political thought, period," Stone stresses. His calm tone betrays the advocacy in what he is saying: "To be clear, Huey Newton is not important because he is a Black Nationalist, though that is one of the things he may be. You will get to explore that question. He is important, given the innovative ways he is thinking about political power, democracy, and Marxism. This is true of all the thinkers we will read." He paces the stage. "I think the value in this course is that it is crucial to all Western political theory." He explains that, to redress the marginalization of these thinkers from the traditional canon, his course will take students through a "systematic, objective appraisal" of their ideas: "In this class, we are going to give these authors and texts the kind of attention that they deserve and require." He then describes this attention as "generous but critical." Stone tells students that "unlike the rest of the world," students should not fall for the trap of trying to judge the ideas outside of their context. Rather, they should give the thinkers their due: "Within the parameters of their ideas, as they lay them out, what are the good aspects of the argument they are making, and what doesn't quite hold up?" Stone is visibly excited by what he is proposing to students. By the time he references that he is teaching the course "for the fifth or sixth time," because it matters so much, students understand. There is a choreography of hands that animates Black speech, and, ever the seasoned practitioner, Stone is cutting the air with his hands, breaking it down: "These ideas are integral to political theory, period. And if you don't know them, then you don't know political thought, simple as that. You just don't."

The two professors could not be more different. Thomas, a working-class White man from Philadelphia, taught American literature. Fond of pairing jeans with his button-down shirts, sleeves rolled up, he once described his teaching style to me as "much more jazz than symphony." Stone, a Black man born and raised solidly middle class in New York City, taught political theory and described his style as "clinical in the sense of trying to have a surgeon's precision and dispassion." Thomas, a self-professed scholar-activist, wore his heart on his sleeve, while Stone kept it tucked in the breast pocket of his three-piece suit. Despite these differences, the commonalities between the two professors' remarks became clear to me when I studied them in hindsight. I understood that both professors had created certain conditions by discussing, from the onset, how content and culture would connect in their courses. Both professors, on the first day, discussed the significance of the content to be learned as well as their expectations for how students should engage with that content and with one another. I came to call this foundational part of the process grounding for learning.

WHAT IS GROUNDING FOR LEARNING?

Grounding for learning is the foundation of the Brave Community method. It is a combination of content and culture that distinguishes learning spaces. I emphasize "for learning" to indicate that we are talking about grounding what learning, specifically, requires. The phrase is meant to conjure an ideal classroom in our minds, though we are not limited to actual classrooms when employing the Brave Community method.

For our purposes, a learning space can be a classroom but also a community room, board room, break room, and, increasingly, a virtual room. Such a space may hold a community of learners that's large or small. Learners may be meeting over 15 weeks, 2 days, or 2 hours. The learners might be college-aged, or middle-aged, or children. Teachers may be classroom teachers, professors, moderators, principals, coaches, managers, community leaders, or community members. They may be anyone who chooses to be responsible for people's learning experience.

The following is a partial list of spaces that are not grounded for learning and, therefore, not the concern of this book: a train, bus, Twitter thread, Facebook page, group chat, rant on Instagram Live or similar social media platform, cable news show, and an unfortunately large number of poorly handled professional development opportunities. This list is clearly not comprehensive but makes the point that, although most social gatherings can be grounded for learning, not all social gatherings actually are. In fact, the most prominent social space that we engage in these days, social media, is devoid of grounding for learning. Yes, people are gathering, sometimes at almost unbelievable rates of speed and scale, as when something or someone goes viral, and, yes, information can be shared. But people on social media are not drawing from common content for learning, as people do in classrooms. Critically, they also are not in agreement about how to productively engage one another. The absence of content and culture for learning means that a space is not grounded for learning.

Content

Content includes not only books, articles, podcasts, films, videos, and all manner of evidence and data, but also the content of a teacher's lectures and of learners' discussions. It comprises, essentially, learning materials. It does not include unfounded opinion. I realize that, in our time, when disinformation runs rampant on the Internet, and what often passes for "news" is just a collection of pundits arguing, it seems futile to try to define content clearly. On the contrary, doing so is essential. I think that discernment about what constitutes content is more critical than ever, particularly when education is for the purpose of relieving or ending an injustice like racism. Freedom comes only by way of telling truth to power, which requires that we stake our claim on what is and is not true. This is becoming increasingly difficult in our "post-truth" climate. No one said, however, that teaching is easy. All learning relies on content, and learning about racism is no exception, no matter how much our politics suggest otherwise.

The content provides solid ground. When we are discussing a reading, a video, or data, we can stand on that ground, which we cannot do with individual feelings and opinions. This doesn't mean that those aspects are not present. Rather, it means that having a clearly delineated content arena to step into frees us to "push ourselves." By identifying the content, we tell learners what they are expected to learn. Simultaneously, they know that their peers are standing on the same ground. I see the content as the sturdy stage on which multiperspective, multiracial learning about racism can take place. In Chapter 4, the Practice chapter, I discuss how to determine how much content we need. The short version is that the content depends on your learning goals and context.

Culture

If content is the solid ground on which learners can stand, culture becomes their common ground. Culture for learning includes ways of being as well as agreed-upon norms for how learners will relate to one another and to the content. A culture that supports learning is widely understood to be familiar to learners from kindergarten on: listening actively, being respectful of others, and speaking in ways that are grounded in what is being taught. I often say that, although such a culture *should* undergird all learning, it *must* be present for productive learning about racism. If a healthy learning culture is missing in a college writing course, or a 10th-grade Algebra class, students may enjoy the class less, but everyone will probably be okay. When that culture is not established for a group that is learning about racism, however, the chances are high that whatever takes place will be unpleasant.

Individuals have limited experience with talking about racism within their community and in public and often harbor anxiety about doing so. Given their experiences with widespread, generational racism, people of color rightly mistrust White people. We anticipate that learning about it will expose us to White peoples' ignorance of racism, at best, and their hostility, at worst. White people rightly fear that people of color will judge them for being the racially dominant group in society. They anticipate tension at best and hostility at worst.

In my teaching experience, I find it compelling that, despite individual diversity, the experience of being grounded empowers *all learners similarly*. A clear sense of what they are learning about racism, and how they are supposed to be engaging with this learning, frees everyone to learn deeply. This experience allows everyone to move along their learning path because they have a clear look at it and can clearly see themselves on it.

A Balance of Content and Culture

In the early stages of the development of the concept of grounding for learning and its role in Brave Community, I had a large investment on what "content" alone could provide. I saw content as kind of an armor. I had a "facts don't care about feelings" approach. One day, when presenting my ideas to teaching assistants in my graduate program, I stressed, with excess harshness and zero nuance, that "emotions do not belong" in the Brave Community method. My still-developing reasoning at the time was that emotional outbursts derail learning, and what doesn't serve learning does not belong in Brave Community. At this point, my self-righteous rant masquerading as teaching was interrupted. Thalía, a friend and fellow graduate student in attendance was talking, and her voice had the sound of impending tears:

> I am feeling so hurt by what you are saying. And so confused. All of this content you are talking about is so painful, and everywhere in society we are asked to tolerate and not show emotion and overcome. And that hurts! And now you're saying emotions, like what I am feeling right now, are not allowed?

My first, unhelpful thought, which I did not share, was, "Great, you're presenting your brand-new pedagogical approach that you say empowers everyone, but especially people of color, to feel like they can have a handle on learning about racism, and Thalía, who is a woman of color, is actually about to cry. Nicely done, Janine."

I remember that I responded to Thalía defensively and poorly, but, mercifully, I don't remember what I said. Afterwards, my wise counsel and friend, Jake, pulled me aside and helped me see what I was saying better than I could see it. "I think what I hear you saying," he said, "is that, when emotions enter, they have to basically become content, they have to be available for learners to take up. Emotions do not replace content, but, if handled that way, they can be part of the content."

Exactly. Grounding for learning, the foundation of the method, is not some magic wand that makes feelings disappear. We are our feelings, and we must honor ourselves by honoring our feelings. Deep learning connects mind and heart, thinking and feeling. The boundary I draw with grounding for learning, however, is around what is primary, what is foundational. For the Brave Community method to work, the priority must be that which grounds everyone in learning and that excludes volatile emotions. As I often remind learners, "I am a Black woman, and I raised a Black child in America. All my rage, all my indignation is righteous. But it does not belong in our learning space." Volatile emotions may be a warranted, or even an inevitable, part of your experience, but they are not grounding for learning. One great way to test whether an emotion or feeling belongs in a Brave Community context is to ask: Does this statement that I am about to make, this feeling I am expressing, and the way I am expressing it, support everyone's learning? If the answer is no, then you are not contributing to that integration of content and culture, that special sauce that is most conducive to learning about racism.

PROFESSOR DE NOVAIS'S FIRST TIME: GROUNDING FOR LEARNING

In the years after I completed my study, the response to my Brave Community workshops or invited talks was overwhelmingly positive. The core idea that productive teaching and learning about racism must be *grounded for learning* resonated deeply with audiences of educators in college and K–12 alike. Every time, they told me that they felt empowered by the accessibility and adaptability of the approach. Despite this public interest and great feedback, when the time came, I was nervous about teaching an entire course, alone, for the first time. What if I, a newbie, could not create and sustain what I was so busy proselytizing? I was clear that "grounding for learning is the foundation of Brave Community." I also was clear that, in my study, Professors Thomas and Stone had established academic grounding through charismatic speeches on their first day of class. But I was no Professor Stone or Thomas. They were both experienced and, given their popularity and positive student evaluations, confident. Their reputations preceded them into classrooms that were full of impressionable undergraduates. In contrast, I was a Black doctoral student, still 5 months shy of graduation, about to enter a classroom full of my difficult-to-impress fellow graduate students. I had never taught alone before, and I had designed the course myself. I was eager to try but not at all confident.

According to my own method, the first thing I had to do was to ground my classroom. Recalling my observational notes on first-day remarks by the two professors, to prepare for my first solo class, I understood what was most crucial about those moments: palpable authenticity. I remembered how both professors infused their remarks with their distinctive personalities, their reasons for doing their work, their aspirations for the class. I remembered feeling how real and connected to their students they felt in those moments. Thomas told the students that he expected them to be respectful of one another, in view of the depth of dehumanization and disrespect that the authors they would read had endured. Stone asked for a generosity of critique because he wanted students to treat Black political thinkers with the respect with which their classical (read: White) counterparts were treated. Both professors, like magicians, had used authenticity to create the grounded community that their students would require.

I understood that I had to do it by being authentic. But what was my authentic teacher self? Who was she? The night before I taught my first class, I journaled about these questions. I thought back about the teachers who had changed my life, who had helped me to learn in transformative ways. Madame C., in the 3rd grade, who had made this bushy-haired Black kid feel like the center of a very White Belgian classroom by always praising my comments, and sometimes even asking me to come up and write them on the board. The way that Susan Szachowicz, my 10th-grade history teacher, humanized Brockton High School—a behemoth to my recently immigrated eyes—by letting me be a protagonist in a history reenactment (Archduke Ferdinand's assassination; I played the wife). The way Lynn Chancer let me, a mere undergraduate, not only take her graduate theory course but also debate a renowned guest speaker. I thought about how learning always made me feel seen.

I traced my steps from a person who, at the start of graduate school, had a deathly fear of public speaking to one who now joyfully gave conference presentations and taught discussion sections. I recollected myriad debates, sober and not, high energy and low, with my colleagues—the aliveness of it all. I recalled how I sat with the challenge of learning to be wrong and engaged in the practice of learning to really listen rather than just wait my turn to speak. I reflected on a lifetime of coming to understand that, at its best, intellectual discussion is not a fight but a creative collaboration. I saw that my long-windedness could break down complex ideas but also devolve into overindulgence. I saw that my sense of humor and colloquialism could charm or turn off, depending on the moment and the person. As I wrote about all of this, I sketched a portrait of myself as a teacher. My thinking about what kind of learner I was revealed what kind of teacher I would be. I was in love with and in awe of learning, but teaching intimidated me. I didn't know everything that I wish I knew, but I knew learning should be joyful, and bring freedom and a sense of belonging.

And so it was that I walked into my first classroom, a beautiful wood-paneled seminar room anchored by a single large table, full of nerves, knowing the teacher I hoped to become. I told the 15 women sitting around the table that I was as thrilled to be there as I was nervous. I told them to get ready for many such unsolicited honest "self-narration" moments from me, as those "make me feel at home, and I need to feel at home to think." The students smiled, and that made me feel welcome. With that, I started.

"I know that courses about race can be uncomfortable, tense, superficial, but I intend for this class to be different." I noticed immediately how everyone nodded, how visibly relieved they seemed that these were my first words. So I walked up to the chalkboard and asked them to join in.

"Actually, you tell me. Tell me the words that come to mind when you think of your previous experiences with courses about race." Students started to shout out words. *Tense, combative, judgmental, rare, one-sided, superficial.* I wrote down what they said, pausing and interjecting to facilitate what had become our first group discussion. "What do you mean by judgmental? What kind of tension? One-sided means what, exactly?" I invited everyone to engage: "Anyone can answer or clarify; it doesn't have to be the person who said the word."

When we had a rich list of almost exclusively unpleasant words, I asked for a different perspective. "Okay, so let's flip this. What word describes ways of being that will help us avoid these common and unpleasant experiences that you've had? What do you think you need for you to be able to learn about race and racism productively?" Luce, a Native woman and the only person of color, brought on the first collective laugh by asking, "What if you never been in a good environment for learning about race, and you, like, have no idea?" I told her it was a very fair point. At that moment, we agreed that words could be aspirational, or gut feelings. "You can give me your best guess!" Students then were allowed to venture further. This was especially productive when they started to parse ideas about safety. Someone said, "Safe," and someone immediately responded, "But safe for who?" Then someone related the common phrase, "Assume best intentions," to which someone replied, "But what if you can't?"

"This is a crucial piece, right?" I pushed. "These norms are about relationships." I wanted them to open the words up and discuss their experiences. "What do we actually mean when we say 'safe'?"

"I think I would need it to feel like people will give me a chance to mess up." When Marianne said this, she looked around the table.

I answered her: "Right, not people, but these folks here. Us, right?" Marianne nodded.

"Okay, so Marianne wants to be able to mess up sometimes. What do we think about that?"

I was happy that the students took some time to respond.

"I think," Luce said, addressing her colleague, "you can. I think we can agree that you can mess up, as long as you can, like, hear the feedback that you did."

"Right, without defensiveness," said Elizabeth, completing the thought. Everyone nodded. I was smiling, happy about where we landed. Then Luce asked me a question.

"What about you, Professor? What do you think safety means? I mean if it's okay to share with us right now."

I smiled at how she phrased it because, all along, I had made it explicit that I would be a silent moderator as they did their work.

I think you are all describing being brave in this class and what you need from one another to be brave. And it sounds like you figured it out. For me, that's what makes you safe—knowing you can be your full selves in here and push yourselves, and your community will have our back. I can't make it "safe," and if I said I could, I'd be lying. But *we* [gesturing as if I could cradle the table and those women in my arms], we can keep *ourselves* safe.

When we were finished with the discussion, I told students that what we had done was to co-imagine our ideal classroom culture, that doing this was necessary because we were going to learn about racism and that would be challenging. "I will need your help in making sure that our community relies on these norms for the semester," I said. "But I promise to keep a watch on that for us." Then, I felt that I needed to say more.

This learning is hard because racism is abhorrent; it is obscene, and it destroys lives, including the lives of students. Listen, I feel like it's one thing that we adults exist in a racist world. It's horrible, but, you know, we're grown adults. But racism infects *classrooms and schools*. And young people, *very young* people, suffer.

Something caught in my throat just then. "There it is," I thought; "This feels real." These words, that I had not planned for, permeated the space around us. My vulnerability, which was now loose in the room, was excruciating.

Racism ruined my son's schooling, from kindergarten on. It's been the hardest, most awful fight of my life, and no amount of education that I have, no matter how hard I have tried, I am no match for that tacit, everyday racism that's baked into schools. Kids like my son, so many kids, suffer in schools. And we keep sending them there. For a majority of their young lives, we make them go places that make them feel less than themselves. [Now I could barely keep from crying.] I think that is unacceptable. So, my son Jalen, kids like him, is why I do this work.

To this day, some version of these remarks, following the collective norms-creating activity, is how I establish grounding for learning in every space I enter, whether a course or workshop. Over the years, I have sometimes included a photo of my son Jalen in my PowerPoint slides to make me feel even more at home, even more connected. Jalen's photo has evolved from one of a sensitive, long-haired, smiling middle-schooler to a self-possessed 22-year-old with cropped hair who smiles only with his eyes. The particular ways that America's racial nightmare rages around me, as I do this work, changes, but the central purpose of the work, for me, is the same. I teach and learn about race to unlearn racism, to help save the kids and their future from White supremacy.

CHAPTER 2

Bravery

PROFESSOR, WHY SHOULD WE CARE ABOUT THEM?

I am in my first year as an assistant professor. My undergraduate class at the School of Education where I teach consists of two Latinas and 33 White women who are all studying to be elementary school teachers. The class racial composition mimics that of the teaching profession nationally, in which roughly 80% of teachers are White women (Taie & Goldring, 2020). I designed this introductory course, which is the program's only required course focused on racial and cultural diversity. My course helps students craft an understanding of what race and culture are before delving into how they interact to produce inequality in education. As I explain to my students, often courses on equity in education skip this foundational step to then study "racial disparities" in education.

The ultimate goal of my course is to teach my students enough about racism so that they will be able to see it working in school practices and policies. The hope is that they will be less likely to inadvertently reproduce racist practices when they become teachers of mostly kids of color. We spent the first 4 weeks on foundational work: What is race? What is culture? How does the cultural and social hierarchy of the wider culture manifest in classrooms and schools? Then we turned to more specific discussions of the challenges that these issues bring to teachers and students alike.

On this day, we are focused on undocumented students and their families. In preparation for class, I assigned my students a *New York Times* article about the college-going struggles of undocumented students who benefited from the Development, Relief, and Education for Alien Minors (DREAM) Act, known colloquially as Dreamers. Passed under President Obama, the DREAM Act permitted certain immigrant students who grew up in the United States without documentation to apply for conditional nonimmigrant status and eventually become eligible for U.S. citizenship if they enrolled in college or served in the U.S. military (Russakoff, 2017). I chose the article in part because one of the students featured was enrolled at a campus in our state; she looked, in the *Times* photos, just like one of my students.

From day one, Alexandra stood out. She always comes prepared, and she is intellectually sharp and creative. She usually cannot wait to share a comment or question, so I am amused at her hesitation today. Alex is the student who volunteered, during our first meeting, that, although she was adopted from Guatemala, she had been "raised very White, really." "I mean, I know I am not White, and I don't look White, but I was adopted and raised by a very White, conservative family." Yet this morning, Alex is clearly unsure of herself when she speaks.

"So, I have, like, a major question," she says, hand raised. "But I know you haven't even started your lecture, so maybe it's not the time?" Before I can answer, Alex answers herself. "But then I really do think it's the kind of question that's about the *whole point* of the class, so I think, uh, I just think, I should maybe ask it now?"

I smile to encourage her. "Oh, come on, Alex, just ask!" Someone echoes me. "Yeah, just ask, and if it's not the right time, she'll tell you." Someone else reminds her, "We said we would be open-minded, and we could be honest, so go for it!" I am pleased to see my Brave Community approach doing what it is supposed to do. Alex takes a mockingly ceremonious big breath and "goes for it."

> Well, almost everything we've learned in this class so far has been new for me. A lot of it has not matched my earlier ideas, or how I was raised, at all. That has been challenging but also fine because I think that is exactly what college is all about. But this assignment was the first time that I felt not just challenged but maybe a little angry? As I was reading the article, I kinda got angry.

As Alex speaks, my heart starts to feel like tin foil being crushed in someone's hand. My hands go icy cold, and I grip the sides of the podium. I am completely caught off guard by what I am hearing. Alex continues, speaking very carefully.

> Okay, so my parents are conservative, but they are good people. They are caring and kind people, and I am a caring person. At least, I think I am. But when reading the article, I kept thinking, "Why should we care about them?" Because the way I was raised, I was taught that these people, they're not citizens. So my question is, I guess, professor, why *should* we care about them?

Around me, there is a sea of mostly White, young faces. Clearly, they all want my answer. Sonia, the only other student of color in the room, who is Latina, looks as hurt and startled as I feel on the inside. I am acutely aware that Sonia also desperately needs to hear my answer. Things start to feel like they are happening too fast for me, like I am running out of breath before I even speak. Somehow, I manage to appear calm and collected on the outside.

"Thank you for being so honest and brave, Alex." I pause to think if I mean that. I do. In the first week of this class, we agreed that ours would be a classroom where people could ask hard questions and make mistakes. What people do not know about racism is the raw material that we work with. Their ignorance is what we work to reduce. Their ignorance is also painful. Alex does not know, but I was undocumented for a period, and, for that reason, I almost did not make it to college. The "them" in Alex's question includes me and my community. Her question is about Sonia's community, about the millions who live in the United States but are undocumented, many of them young people who know no other home. Most challenging of all, it is the kids whom the government is holding in cages at the Southern border. The faces looking at me bring me back with their look that says, "Go ahead, *professor*. Answer the question."

> I am grateful for Alex's honesty. But you know, as someone who is an immigrant and who was once undocumented myself, like the Dreamers, the question hurt my feelings, you know? It would hurt anyone who is or has loved ones who are undocumented, and that could be any number of us.

I look intentionally but discreetly at Sonia when I say this. I reassure the students that, despite the difficulty, Alex's question is an honest one, and one we have to be able to ask as a means to finding the answer. "I think I need to cover some ground that I was not planning to cover today, to better contextualize Alex's question."

Then I freestyle a lecture. I cover the founding of the United States, settler colonialism, Manifest Destiny, immigration, and work permit laws over the years, and how the United States is the notorious original border crosser, as well as the continuous economic exploitation of Mexico and other nations by developed nations. None of this is prepared, and I know I am covering too much too fast, but everyone seems engrossed in the moment, so I know that I am making enough sense. When I wrap up, I ask the students to spend the rest of the class discussing, in small groups, how they would help Alex answer her question, given the information that I just shared.

They dive right in. I walk around the room, where they sit five to a table. I listen to make sure that they are on task. They periodically ask me to clarify: Was the border ever open? If it's so risky, why do people come over the border? Are the requirements for Dreamers still in place, or did Trump end the policy? Are there Dreamers at our university? When class ends, the students give me smiling "thank yous" as they trickle out. Alex stops by the podium to check in. We exchange a knowing look that, for me, at least, means, "Whew, that was *a lot*." She speaks first.

> Knowing more about the border and everything, I can really see that it's not so cut and dry as how I was thinking. I did not know any of this, I mean, except for "Manifest Destiny"—we did cover that in high school. Thank you for taking the time to explain it all to us even though you didn't plan to do it.

I thank her again, especially for giving us "the context about your family and where your question was coming from. I know that took a lot of courage." She nods and smiles as she backs out of the classroom. When the last student leaves the room, and I am finally alone, I put my head down on the podium. There is sweat dripping down my back. My pulse is loud in my throat.

Later that day, on the train back home, even after debriefing the class with a close colleague, I was still in a bit of a fog. I felt grateful that, despite the emotionality of the moment for me, the simplicity of the Brave Community method made it easy for me to follow it. By following the method, I was able to see *bravery* in Alex's question, a genuine desire to learn that pushed her to take a risk. I could also recognize that the hurtful blow dealt by Alex's question was related to what she did not know but wanted to understand. With that, I knew that my job was to guide our community through that moment, so that we could keep learning.

Her bravery also helped me to see that I had engaged the class in a discussion about undocumented students that assumed that they had an understanding of the background for such a complex discussion, when they did not. Alex's question reminded me that most of my students, and most people, are grounded only in what they learn informally about racism from inadequate K–12 education curricula, family, news, and social media. Time and again, when something happens that is emotionally challenging, which is often the case, the difference between maintaining productive learning and going off the rails is razor thin. Simply referring to the Brave Community method allowed me to ground myself, and then to ground my learners. The method helps us to find our way.

WHAT IS BRAVERY?

Bravery, in the context of the Brave Community method, is a learner's capacity to engage with the tension, risk, and mindset change that learning about racism requires. In practice, it looks like asking difficult questions, hearing difficult answers, letting go of long-held assumptions, and following one's reasoning to new, often uncomfortable conclusions. It takes bravery to change one's mind because all change involves loss. When my student said the article made her angry, I heard her sense of loss. She was angry at the loss of the certainty that her family was kind and loving, even if they did not consider that we should care about undocumented youth and families. Learning is a risk we take in trading what we know for new knowledge.

Learners' bravery propels their own learning but also the learning of the collective: Difficult questions prompt difficult answers, honesty sparks honesty. The bravery elicited through the method is essential because it broadens the learning space. A brave question shines a light into corners of racial ignorance that otherwise stay out of sight. That bravery shows us, often painfully, where and what we need to wade into in order to learn.

My course syllabus changed after that semester to include a lot more background information. Not only was the undocumented student unit preceded by learning the history of U.S. colonial expansion and self-serving immigration laws, but I also made sure to add additional scaffolding to nearly all of the topics. My students' bravery also showed me early on that, although everyone in the course was opinionated about matters of race, when asked, "If you had to, could you define race?" *none of them* answered affirmatively. I therefore added another week to the time we spent on the social construction of race in the United States. My students' honest and risky questions helped me to recognize what they needed to learn above and beyond what I assumed.

Although each moment and person is different, I have observed two consistent ways that bravery appears most often: when students ask the dangerous but necessary question (like Alex did) and when they explicitly connect racism and whiteness.

The Bravery to Ask the Dangerous but Necessary Question

This type of bravery is probably the most common. When learning about racism, learners will come to a fork in the road. In one direction is a risky question that what they are learning elicits—such as, in Alex's case, Why should we care about the rights of undocumented people? In the other direction is comfortable silence. Only an inner voice speaks there:

Maybe someone else will ask my question.

I don't trust these people. They're going to take my question the wrong way.

I don't trust this teacher. She's not going to have my back.
I should know the answer, and it's embarrassing that I don't.
It's not worth it.

When the brave question cannot be asked, the range of learning becomes limited to only what the teacher can or dares to teach. This is bad not only for the learner who stays silent but also for everyone. If Alex doesn't ask me why we should care, I miss the opportunity to answer a fundamental question that was likely in the minds of many students who were raised to believe citizenship rights are decoupled from U.S. history, colonization, and racial oppression. Most of the time, a risky question does have a sound, evidence-based, well-founded answer. If such a question is asked, learners have the opportunity to gain new information, but more importantly, they witness the teacher answering a question that they thought could not be answered.

In a racist world, "wrong answers" are all around. What learners do not learn about how racism works leaves room for racist thinking to take root in their minds. "If you observe a racist world without an understanding of how it works," I remind learners often, "you may start to draw racist conclusions. You may assume there is something about people of color themselves that produces consistently bad outcomes for them." Better to ask the risky question than assume falling prey to the wrong answer.

The race framework that we all carry around by virtue of being socialized in a racist society is termed *racial conceptualization* by sociologist Ann Morning (2009). She defines racial conceptualization as a "complex of beliefs" or a web of ideas about what race is. More than just a definition, racial conceptualization is "effectively a working model of race, one that helps us make sense" in our racialized world (Morning, 2009, p. 1168). Our racial conceptualization orients us as we navigate our lives, and we become attached to it. Testing it and asking it questions, as learning about racism asks us to do, takes will and bravery.

The Bravery to Connect Racism to Whiteness

In 2021, right-wing pundits and media figures launched a coordinated misinformation campaign, suggesting that elementary-age children were being taught *critical race theory* (CRT) in schools. The anti-CRT movement was essentially a movement against the teaching of any facts about the history or contemporary reality of racism in the United States. Schools, libraries, and school boards across the country were overrun by (mostly but not only) White parents protesting any instruction about race or racism. At an elementary school where I was invited to deliver a professional development session, some parents had even removed their children from classes to protest the history curriculum. The group of teachers gathered in the cafeteria for my talk were eager to listen and outspoken about the impossible conditions that they were working under.

The professional development session was going extremely well. I taught the teachers about the invention of American racism as a means to justify the genocide of Native Americans and the enslavement of Africans. We talked about Thomas Jefferson as a model of the core contradiction in the nation's founding. The teachers shared individual stories of difficult confrontations with parents who accused them of teaching CRT. We discussed some next steps that they could take, using the Brave Community approach in upcoming Columbus Day–related lessons.

Happy with all that we had accomplished, I moved to some closing remarks. "So we understand why some people would not want young people to learn this history, right?" Everyone nodded.

> But we also understand that we live in the reality that this history created, so folks need to understand this reality if they stand any chance of changing it. Our young people need the information so they can understand how racism affects their lives. They are dealing with racism, so they need to know how to deal with it, right?

More nods. "So let me ask one of those obvious questions: Who benefits from this history not being taught?"

Suddenly, and for the first time, there was complete silence. The few Black teachers were making eye contact with me, but their eyes seemed to be telling me, "When you leave, we still work here, so you're on your own, sis." A contingent of three that had been ignoring me politely all along, sitting in the back, were doing so more aggressively now, scrolling through their phones.

"Come on, folks. Don't make me do that teacher thing you all do to your kids where you walk over, hover, and ask, 'Who knows the answer?'" They laughed, but no hands were raised. After 30 very long seconds, someone said, "People who are more conservative?"

"Conservative? Okay, in what way?" The young woman who had spoken nudged her colleagues at her table. One of them spoke: "People who don't want . . . change?"

"Okay, yes," I smiled. "Can you say a bit more, be more specific?" The teacher continued, carefully: "Well, if you know something is wrong, you become accountable for making change. So some people prefer we don't talk about what's wrong." Teachers around the room nodded. I took that as a good sign that maybe we could move past this last-minute lack of bravery. I pushed.

"Let me ask again. What's wrong with change for the better? Who wouldn't want us to change how racism affects our lives? Who benefits from that not changing?" To my dismay, the awkward silence returned as if it never left. Then someone timidly raised her hand. I commended her for her bravery. "Older people?" she ventured.

One thing about me is that, at some point, I will laugh, especially when I'm exhausted, so I did. I laughed out loud, and the group did as well.

"Wait." I stopped my laughter, and they stopped theirs. "Are y'all *really* not saying it?" Dismayed, I continued.

> I am going to state the obvious, since you won't. The folks who benefit from no change in a racist society, who benefit from children not learning about how racism was created and works, are people who benefit from racism. Those are the people on top of the racial hierarchy. So, that's White people.

Beverly Tatum's landmark book, *Why Are All the Black Kids Sitting Together in the Cafeteria?,* originally published in 1997, is a classic distillation of this phenomenon. Tatum expertly identifies the destructive effect of our generalized lack of courage to confront issues of racism in community. She describes distinct ways that people of color and White people experience this fear. She also describes the commonalities in how everyone experiences this fear, stating that everyone is threatened by the possible loss of belonging and the possibility of being misunderstood or ostracized that comes with stating that White people benefit from racism. Beneath everyone's skin, this fear is ever ready to be activated, and a racist society knows how to activate it. I could sense it in that cafeteria, and I sense it often.

The stakes were clearly different for the White teachers, who were in the majority, than for the five Black teachers and the Black principal. Nevertheless, for that moment, the fear was practically speaking, the same; the fear was a wall dead smack in the middle of everyone's learning path. After the global antiracist uprisings of 2020, Tatum's book (1997/2017) was once again a national best seller, confirming that we are still "looking for the words," and still afraid.

All around us, we see leaders who fail to rise to the occasion or do so but are immediately shut down. In 2014, then Attorney General Eric Holder faced enormous backlash for stating that, in terms of the discourse on racism, America was a nation of cowards. In his first address to Congress in 2021, after campaigning on a promise to confront structural racism head on, President Joe Biden stated that his policies would "root out systemic racism that plagues America." By the next day, he was on television, providing a defensive answer to the question of whether he thought the United States was a racist country (Naylor, 2021).

> No, I don't think the American people are racist. But I think after 400 years, African Americans have been left in the position where they're so far behind the eight ball in terms of education, health, in terms of opportunity. (para. 5)

All it took to get this backpedaling was Republican Senator Tim Scott, in his televised response, stating, as a matter of opinion, not fact, "America is not a racist country" (Naylor, 2021, para. 3).

We have been consistently called to be braver. In 2008, Singleton and Hays's Courageous Conversations framework posited that productive discussions about racism must lean on courage and accept open-ended discomfort (Singleton & Hays, 2008). Their framework is widely used in educational and cultural settings beyond the United States to this day. Scholars Arao and Clemens argued in 2013 that the ubiquity of "safe space" as a goal for learners detracted from the courage necessary for real transformative work on racism to occur. In response, Arao and Clemens proposed the now popular idea of *brave space* that makes clear "the need for courage, rather than the illusion of safety" (p. 141). Entrepreneur Mellody Hobson's 2014 TED talk, viewed almost a million times, asks corporate leaders to eschew the colorblindness that has come to characterize DEI efforts and, instead, to be "color brave," or intentional about producing racially diverse and equitable workplaces. In 2017, world-renowned scholar and author Brené Brown wrote about being honest about Donald Trump's racism in a book titled *Braving the Wilderness*.

Much was made of the "racial reckoning" that we seemed poised to have in 2020. Many expected the aftermath of the global protests to be times of brave confrontation with White supremacy worldwide. In the United States, however, as soon as the backlash hit, the reckoning became a muzzling. The right wing attacked antiracist work everywhere, in ways that transcended critical race theory bans, and pushed back even the intention of asking brave questions.

This national cowardice about engaging with racism comes, in part, from not being grounded when we approach the issue. In spaces where we are not grounded for learning yet are asked to think and learn about racism, we do not know who we are in the room with. Even within racially homogeneous groups, let alone in mixed racial company, our diversity of experience and sense-making is infinite. This open-ended possibility for tension exacerbates the anxiety that learners already feel around broaching the topic of racism. So even though we know that we should be brave, we generally do not dare to be. The Brave Community method is a direct response to the fact that it is not enough to prescribe bravery or denounce its absence. We need a reliable mechanism to support learners to develop bravery. That mechanism is grounding for learning.

By now, many of you are asking a question that, in some form or another, I get all of the time: "But isn't someone's bravery another person's microaggression?"[1] Notably, the Brave Community method attends to the context that is ideal for learning about racism. One aspect of that context, which we turn to in the next chapter, is that the bravery that learners demonstrate and express is received by their community with spaciousness, trust, and generosity. The bravery is in a dynamic balance with what I call *resilient empathy*. (Dynamic balance is a phrase for which I thank my colleague Malik Muhammad.)

CHAPTER 3

Resilient Empathy

It is simply not true that unless I have undergone the exact same experience as the other, I know nothing about his or her pain and should simply shut up. Insofar as to be human is to open oneself up to the possibility always already there of becoming (an)other, such a conception of self and identity is by definition antihuman. The political in our time must start from the imperative to reconstruct the world in common.

—Achille Mbembe (cited in Nilsen, 2019)

Resilient empathy, the third and final component of Brave Community, the counterpart to bravery, is the ability to put oneself in someone else's shoes even when their expressed thoughts create initial discomfort or distrust in us. Empathy is integral to learning because it is what allows us to consider and then learn from points of view other than our own. I modify it with the word "resilient" to emphasize that, in the case of learning about racism, empathy can be the hardest work. One learner's leap of intellectual bravery requires other learners' resilient empathy, or their "brave listening," as a safety net.[1] Learners extend this empathy for others because they understand that they will need the same themselves if they are to feel capable of taking risks. At the most basic level, the word "resilient" is meant to highlight that learners have to wade through a lot of resistance and distraction to arrive at and maintain this kind of empathy. In order to do this hard work, learners need support. Like the bravery it complements, resilient empathy is not naturally occurring or incidental, it also relies on grounding for learning. During my study of Charles Thomas's class, one of his students, Lyor, put it this way:

> You respect people. You let them say what they want to say, and you try and take it and analyze on that [intellectual] level. It creates a level of comfort, where you can misspeak like Kevin misspeaks, and I don't think anybody thinks he's a racist because he misspoke, whereas, if he said things in a different context, it could be more problematic.

When he told me this, Lyor was reflecting on a particular moment during Thomas's class that I would like to share with you.

QUESTIONS THAT RAISE OUR BLOOD PRESSURE

It was the penultimate meeting of the course, and, by then, Thomas's classroom was a well-oiled machine. Evans, a student, noted, "Everyone brings their whole selves," and students disagreed strongly but without acrimony. As Warner, another student, stated, they had become so close as to be able to guess "what other people [are] going to say when they raise their hands."

The two students who were discussion leaders for that week opened with the following question: "What is the place of violent rebellion in slavery?" I observed that students did not jump in as they usually did. Slowly, a couple of students commented that all violence is abhorrent. A few others asked whether a turn to violence is ever justified. Students spoke in short sentences and did not sound very confident. Their body language—avoiding eye contact, emitting audible sighs, exchanging judging looks with a fellow classmate while another is speaking—showed an uncharacteristic tension in the room, and Kevin and Evans's exchange escalated.

> Kevin: I think we are not looking critically at Turner's inhumanity.
> Evans: What inhumanity?
> Kevin: He enjoys the violence! He's having a good time! He's a sociopath!
> Evans: That's a word that shuts down the debate! You're taking Turner out of his context and putting his actions in a vacuum!

Evans accused Kevin of speaking without any concern for context, "in a vacuum." Others agreed with the "sociopath" comment. Kevin was visibly frustrated in his attempts to assert that he was not ignoring context. It was as if things were just too heavy to push forward. The violence of Nat Turner's rebellion 180 years ago was a ghost made flesh in the classroom.

It was Fall 2014 when, one hashtag at a time, we routinely confronted the shooting deaths of unarmed Black people at the hands of police. When summer protests erupted, some called them riots. It was difficult for students to engage in a text that centers the violence of slavery at a time when the violence of contemporary racism loomed. But none of what I was thinking, and what I imagined everyone was thinking, was being said. I realized that learning about race can be difficult no matter what level of pedagogical or intellectual prowess is in the room; it is difficult because racism, and related ideas, such as antiracist violence, are difficult to confront. The class fell completely silent. After a couple of awkward minutes, Thomas abruptly rose from the seminar table and paced over to the wall. He laughed quietly and spoke to no one in particular: "You know, I walked up here as if there was a dry-erase board to write on, because I just needed something to do, and there isn't!" Everyone laughed, and, with the silence broken, Thomas continued:

> I know this is really hard. But the fact that it is hard doesn't mean we stop. It just means we work harder. The reality is we often want our revolutions to be neat, to be without violence, and they're just not. We construct ideas about crime and violence as immoral, but isn't slavery immoral, isn't it one big crime scene? These questions that raise our blood pressure around the table are the point of this class.

Lyor immediately recognized that Thomas was asking the group to re-engage. He was asking them to override the temptation to take the easy way out, a simple two-sided view: "We get it; they don't." Lyor started to build a bridge by explaining his side better. "I don't think we're here to judge Nat Turner specifically. Whether he was crazy or not, I think we should consider the bigger issue of revolt and what does it take to resist." This effort on Lyor's part suggested to those listening that he found them worthy of this bridging effort.

Kevin continued in this mode, working to express himself better than he did earlier. "My comment about him being a sociopath was less about the violence, the ends, and more about his means. I just don't want us to let him off the hook." Evans nodded and suggested that their disagreement may in fact be about something more nuanced. "We are disagreeing about the difference between how we see systemic violence and individual violent acts."

In each of these turns of discussion, the learner was pushing past treating disagreement as a given, past distrust, and entering the space of another's perspective. It was a form of speaking that says, "I can pretend otherwise, but I actually recognize how you might be misunderstanding me, and I am going to try to put it in a way you can grasp." This was empathy as hard work. Adina spoke next:

> You think Nat Turner is crazy because [of what he does and how he thinks]. But with the system of slavery, so many people bought into a crazy system of violence. Yes, it horrified me to hear about him talking about killing babies, but why was I desensitized to all the dead babies that slavery produced?

Following Adina, Jessica was comfortable enough to think aloud: "Nat Turner's heroism is kind of . . . filthy, and we don't know, as Americans, how to deal with this. How do I stand on the shoulders of a Nat Turner like I stand on the shoulders of an MLK?"

Deyanira then offered the conclusion, and I thought, sitting in the corner, that she said what they were all thinking. "But you do, right? We already do."

As I watched the students, who not long ago were in a hostile moment, now speak freely, trusting that they can be understood, I realized that the empathy they were extending to one another propelled their discussion to more depth. The balance of the resilient empathy and bravery augmented what was possible for them. Thomas's student, Lyor, conveyed this sense of agency clearly in his comments above. He described *a choice* to extend his understanding to a colleague who "misspeaks," in the service of everyone's learning.

Resilient empathy is not experienced as a superimposed burden but as an act of deliberate participation.

Resilient empathy is a contingent relationship among learners that has parameters. Yes, it is okay for Kevin to misspeak in the service of his learning, in this class, in this community, where others are in community with him, whereas elsewhere, as Lyor understood, "It could be more problematic."

Over the years, my students have often highlighted this experience of making one another's learning possible through resilient empathy. Cass, who was a student in one of my graduate courses, stated:

> We were able to let each other be vulnerable, and I think an academic classroom is not often seen as a place of vulnerability. I think when people say vulnerable, they think of tears and crying and sadness. But I think the vulnerability was more so about possibly being wrong about a subject, racism, that is very heated and very topical and very difficult to discuss for many folks, and having peers support you to do that. I think, despite our diverse backgrounds, we were able to come together as a unit and find ways to support each other in that way.

We often discuss how being teachable, having an intellectual humility, is important to learning, and it is. But there is, as Cass describes, a great vulnerability as well in learning about racism because the stakes are so high. Resilient empathy makes space for the vulnerability that comes with intellectual bravery.

THE CHALLENGE OF RESILIENT EMPATHY IN A RACIST WORLD

Resilient empathy is the component of the Brave Community method that meets with the most resistance, or outright rejection, in my experience. This makes sense. There is no question that teaching and learning about

racism presents a particular challenge for empathy. There are several related reasons for this. To learn about racism means to intentionally and
specifically bring it up. Racism, the systematic and longstanding injury of
people of color for the advantage of White people, is a grave and painful
injustice to confront. People of color, who have been historically victim-
ized by racist oppression, and continue to experience it, have reason to
mistrust and resent White people. It is difficult for them to feel empathy for
White people. White people know the distrust and resentment that people
of color have of them. They often deny that they are personally at fault for
racism and the suffering of others. They resent and do not empathize with
people of color's perspective to the contrary.

Research consistently shows gaps in empathy that fall across racial
lines as well as the preponderance of low trust in cross-racial interaction
(Bobo et al., 2012; Richeson & Shelton, 2007; Shelton & Richeson, 2006;
Sorensen et al., 2009). We live in a racist society that seeks to sustain itself in part by keeping the cross-racial empathy gap as wide as possible.
Unfortunately, we often think that, because resilient empathy is difficult to
find or even fathom, it is impossible to achieve. The worst part is that we
do not just passively walk away from empathy; we distort it.

Far from authentic empathy, what often predominates in our culture
is a distortion of empathy into "parking lots for emotionality and white
fragility, recentering whiteness and irrationally requiring people of color
to bear witness to these emotions" (Patel, 2016, p. 83). The most recent
surge of this happened in the wake of Donald Trump's election. Although
the moment produced a seriously hostile environment for people of color,
with the racist and xenophobic tenor of Trump's campaign and persona,
mainstream media and social science discourse called for more empathy
for the Trump voter. Two examples are the 2016 best-selling memoir by
J. D. Vance, *Hillbilly Elegy*, which became a major motion picture, and
the 2018 sociological study by Arlie Hochschild, *Strangers in Their Own
Land: Anger and Mourning on the American Right*.

There was a powerful call to better understand the nuanced ways in
which the racial resentment expressed by Trump voters interacted with
cultural alienation or socioeconomic issues. But there was no equivalent
desire to understand the precarity that the majority of people whose ac-
cidents of birth put them in jeopardy in the America envisioned by the
45th president: people of color, immigrants, Muslims, LGBTQIA+ individuals, disabled people, and those at the intersections of these identities.

Another example of this distorted sense of empathy is the phenomenon of educators, usually in elementary schools, who stage situations in
which learners or staff are supposed to "feel like" someone else, usually a
person of color, or someone else deemed to be marginalized. News stories
about awful examples of this can easily be found on Google. To cite one

of numerous examples, in 2022, some 4th-grade teachers asked students to "Write a letter to President Andrew Jackson from the perspective of an American settler and explain why removing the Cherokee will help the United States grow and prosper" (Schilling, 2022).

Although White people are overrepresented in these unfortunate-to-abhorrent incidents, people of color also participate. Some of the administrators who put their entire staff through poverty simulations, a kind of scripted group activity in which staff act out roles based on the most reductive and offensive stereotypes of poor people, are people of color. The premise of all these activities is that people of color, low-income people, or, more generally, people different from oneself can be understood only through playacting.

Another distorted empathy premise is that people of color are incapable of empathy toward White people and should not be expected to have it. We conclude, unrealistically, that it is an undue burden to ask students of color to show resilient empathy. I find this misguided for three reasons. First, in my experience, learners of color are able and willing to express resilient empathy in the appropriate context. Second, presuming to know what "all students of color" might or might not be able or willing to do is essentialist. Third, resilient empathy is a requirement for learning. If learning is the goal, excluding students of color from what learning requires is to implicitly exclude them from the learning community. It exacerbates their marginalization rather than reduce it.

Resilient empathy is not to be donned like a costume or learned like a pledge of allegiance. We humans are wired for empathy. Our neurology, our brains, rely on our built-in ability to consider another person's perspective. Barring actual sociopathy, we can all connect with what deprivation, fear, and oppression feel like. I despair whenever White parents say to me, "I can't imagine what it is like" to fear that my son might be killed by police. I could dismiss it as a clumsy attempt at empathy, but it is too clearly an illustration of a deeper problem. If individuals are parents, of course they have despaired at their child's slightest discomfort, their first bad stomach virus, toothache, or broken bone. They know exactly what it must be like for me to fear for my child's physical safety. That the terror that I know so well is completely far-fetched for them doesn't mean that they cannot fathom it. Being unwilling to empathize across racial or other social differences is different from being unable.

Spaces full of empathy and empty of bravery are not conducive to learning. There is a preponderance of antiracist work that is done in this way. Participants make room for feelings but are are not required to learn and be productively challenged by knowledge about racism. Conversely, as the story below shows, no real learning or growth happens in spaces full of bravery and empty of resilient empathy.

RESILIENT EMPATHY AS A RIGHT AND A DUTY

I am leading a group of schools selected by their state department of education to participate in a daylong "race and equity" professional development session. The schools, a mix of urban and suburban, all struggle with achievement gaps between White students and their Black and Latinx counterparts. In the morning, I hold a Brave Community workshop, during which we learn about the need to be grounded for learning, beginning with a deep discussion of our norms and aspirations for our group. As is always the case, the group sketches a wonderful and ambitious vision for the kind of community that they want to be.

On the blackboard behind me, as we gather after the lunch break, are our "community values": open-minded, honest, teachable, frank, not defensive, focused on the kids, confidential, and kind. The afternoon session begins with a focus on the history and contemporary reality of racism in education. I speak for about 20 minutes and invite participants to freely interrupt and ask questions. Then they have their first small-group discussion break. They are seated in tables of five to eight colleagues, all from the same school. Some groups have their principal with them, and some do not. The group is majority White, but one table has a group of all Black women. Another has all Black and Latinx staff. From the very first moment that I arrived earlier in the day, the Black women were exceedingly warm and happy to see me. They complimented me on my outfit and helped me to warm up the entire room in the morning session, participating actively and helping me to break the ice. This intentional solidarity that Black women extend to one another is familiar and a delight.

I think it's going well when, to my surprise, a voice speaks up before the small-group time is up. As I scan the larger hotel conference room to locate the speaker, I hear the hostility in her voice. I finally spot Marjorie, a White woman who is a bilingual teacher from Spencer High School in Massachusetts. The colleagues at her table look very uncomfortable. Marjorie says, "I'm sorry, but you said we should be brave and say the things we need to say. So I'm gonna do it!" I nod as I walk toward her table and smile. "Absolutely, go ahead."

Well, I am incredibly frustrated because I came here really to learn about solutions for my kids. And I was sharing with my group the problem of when, as a White teacher, I had to discipline a student, and then I do, and the parent complained that it was a racial thing. You know, this mother said that it was a race issue in my class and that is why the young woman was struggling. It wasn't! Her child was just a behavior problem. But the mom said it's race. So, I asked the group, we were discussing what should happen, and I disagreed with Lynette [a colleague].

At this point, I realize why her colleagues are uncomfortable. Marjorie continues.

> My colleague Lynette here said I was wrong, and I really disagree. It wasn't about that. And to be honest, it's been half a day and all we are getting is race, race, race, and, you know, that is not the priority all the time. It's always like this at these trainings. And for some students, there's other issues. My students are Latino and Cape Verdean kids, and their issues have nothing to do with race!

As I am getting ready to respond to Marjorie, standing close to her as I like to do when someone is getting tense, Cori, a Black woman, starts to speak. Cori is part of a team of all Black and Latinx educators from a relatively new charter school in Dorchester. She and her colleagues are the youngest educators in the room, ranging from their late twenties to their early thirties. Cori looks young but she seems mighty. She also sounds hurt and angry. She is not looking at Marjorie and speaks calmly. "It is frankly hurtful that, after a mere *twenty or so* minutes of talking about racism in a serious way, on *the first* day, my colleague already has had enough and is frustrated. You know?"

"I'm sorry, but," Marjorie begins to speak, but I signal for her to wait. Cori continues, and I can tell she is struggling to be calm.

> On top of how hurtful and frustrating it is that she said she's tired of talking about race, she actually should consider that she shouldn't dismiss the parent. Because she could be biased in ways that are not obvious to her. Racist things could be happening, in how she's behaving or handling the class and her students that she's not aware of as a White woman. I mean, did she reflect? Does she have problems with students a lot? How does the young woman do with other teachers? She's not supposed to just dismiss it, I mean, isn't that why we're here?

Marjorie does not wait to respond. Her tone is authoritative. "That's ridiculous. I'm sorry, but it's just not what happened."

I see that Cori is done talking because she is done being able to handle this moment calmly, and I do not blame her. In the moment, I recognize that I am being called to extend resilient empathy to Marjorie, empathy that I *do not* want to extend due to her behavior. Because the source of my resilient empathy is our grounding for learning, however, I orient myself, and

hopefully my group, back to learning. I raise my hand, which is my univer-
sal way of hushing the low volume whispering that's taken over the room.
"Does everyone remember our discussion this morning about grounding
for learning? Who can look at their notes and tell me what that is?"

Adrienne, who is seated with Cori, is eager to help. "Grounding is
that combination of culture and content for learning. So, for us, it's like,
the norms we have on the wall over there and the content you and all the
speakers are sharing."

> Perfect, thank you Adrienne. The first thing I want to say is that
> what I was teaching, Marjorie, was exactly this: the background
> content that we need to have meaningful discussions about all the
> equity issues people are facing, including your specific ones.

Marjorie moves her mouth as if to speak again, and I raise my hand,
faster this time, to clarify that I am not to be interrupted.

> The fundamental mechanism of inequality in the United States is a
> mix of race and class, put together. But that system, what we have
> today, originates in slavery, so an understanding of this early history
> is necessary to understand inequality in the States, including what
> faces immigrant communities of color. One problem is that Marjorie
> and Cori do not share a common definition of the word "racist."
> And Marjorie's definition is incorrect, and Cori's is correct. A school
> can have racist practices and policies in place that feel normal,
> especially when staff are not trained to recognize them. Often,
> teachers are White and do not experience racial discrimination
> themselves, so they are even more prone to miss it. That is what Cori
> was suggesting.

First, I reminded the group of our grounding for learning, then I made explicit how a lack of common grounding—how they understand the word
"racist"—was part of the challenging moment between Marjorie and Cori.
I turn my attention to Marjorie again.

> If you, Marjorie, had that understanding, a better understanding,
> you would have taken the parent's claim seriously. But another
> important problem, Marjorie, is that Cori was very brave and
> generous in letting you know that what you said was hurtful. She
> made that offering, and you did not receive it with kindness. You
> dismissed it, right? And earlier this morning, we said we'd be a
> community that values staying kind even when things were tough.
> So, you have to do better.

With this comment, I make sure that Marjorie was also accountable for not extending resilient empathy to her colleague Cori. I circle back to the grounding for learning that we discussed earlier. Then I am ready to wrap this up. I have now moved away from Marjorie's table and am looking at the full room back behind my table at the front. "Okay, if there are no more questions, let me get us back on track because what we'll cover is related to this."

I think that I have handled this moment, but I see that all the Black and Latinx people in the room seem to have closed up. They stare at their laptops, avoid my eye contact, and cross their arms. Their energy washes over me; it is the feeling of unfinished business. I see that the entire room is tense. We are not done processing yet. I start to pace from one end of the room to the other, with my two fingers placed on my throat, taking my pulse:

Whew! I don't know about you all, but I am feeling this tension right now. Right? My hands are cold, too. This is uncomfortable. And I see something interesting. All the people of color seem turned way off. Right? Y'all are crossing your arms, looking away, not giving me any eye contact, staring down at your laptops, bracing. Right? What is that about? What just happened to the room? Let's hear from someone we've not heard from yet.

Gwendolyn, one of the women at the all-Black table, raises her hand:

I think we're all thinking, you know, it's the same over and over again. People don't want to be accountable to the reality, and they come to sessions like this and always want to push back and challenge the speaker and make excuses. And it's just so predictable, and it's exhausting. I think that's what we're all feeling.

Denva, who was an early source of humor in the morning session, chimes in with a humorous comment. "What Gwendolyn *really* means is the woman acted like a Karen, and we're tired of the Karens!" Then they belly laugh, and this seems to defuse the tension that they and other people of color are holding. A very few White people laugh, too, but most are stone-faced. I make an exasperated-teacher face and walk over to their table. I am smiling, so they know that it's not a real scolding; rather, it is a necessary intervention. "Now, see? Why did y'all have to say that? Y'all gonna make me have to come over there."

The Black women giggle like pretend school children in trouble with the pretend teacher whom I am playing in our impromptu skit. We smile at one another as I approach them. "You're not in trouble, but we must think about the impact of that joke. What did we discuss earlier about resilient empathy?" Cori raises her hand, ready to speak again. "It's being able to put yourself in someone else's shoes. The kind of empathy that's hard work, that you don't want to give someone." I thank her and turn back to the entire group. "Now, can we see how Marjorie's comment failed that empathy mark?" All the women nod strongly. Across the room, it is the same, except for those at Marjorie's table, who nod slightly. I continue, "But what about Denva's joke?" Denva and Gwendolyn look at each other, chuckle again, compose themselves, and get serious. Denva speaks to concede the point:

> No, it really wasn't empathetic, either. I mean, look, being a Karen is a thing, and *it is* annoying that she did do that. But like you said, we are here to do better, and earlier we committed to do better, so we can work together and learn. So it wasn't that resilient empathy, no.

Before I say anything, Gwendolyn asks a question. "Okay, but how do I know I'm doing resilient empathy?" At this, I nod and smile at her and her whole table and wink to thank them for helping me to reset the course of the group. I walk back to the front of the room. "That is a deep question. Thank you, Gwendolyn. So, folks, what do you think? How can you tell you are using that resilient empathy?" The group looks at me, asking, so I offer what I know.

> Honestly, I think you feel it. You can tell what the easy way out is when you take it in a moment like this. What costs little or nothing and what takes more heart or work, right? That easy, gotcha, payback feeling that came with the joke, that's delicious, right?

Everyone laughs. "I know, I know! We're all human. But what's delicious for the ego is not *nutritious*!" More laughs at my corny joke. The key point is to name, in the most honest way possible, how we all understand what Denva did and why it felt good to do it, and yet it was not productive for everyone's learning. I continue to scan the room to see whether everyone is getting this, and they seem to. To my surprise, Marjorie speaks: "I think it was definitely the easy way out for me to be the Karen." Everyone chuckles, as Marjorie continues.

> It was easy to get defensive and make it all about me and my school and my kids and how my needs aren't being met and, even frankly, to challenge you because the morning session made me uncomfortable and, yeah, defensive. Because not getting validation at my table was unpleasant, and I did the easy thing for me. So when Cori spoke, I doubled down.

RESILIENT EMPATHY HAS A SOURCE

I thought a lot about whether to share this story. I was concerned that it would be picked apart and misinterpreted. I included it because it did happen, and similar things have happened often in my work. It is important in these moments that I hold all learners to a standard of resilient empathy. The fact that it is difficult to meet that standard is the point. Just as it was necessary to support Cori for her brave intervention when Marjorie was out of line, it was necessary to be honest about how the "Karen" joke also failed the empathy test in our context. This is not a matter of equivalence at all. It is a Brave Community matter only: Both behaviors, for different reasons and to very different degrees, failed to meet our agreed-upon norms from the morning; both behaviors punctured the Brave Community bubble that we had just created for our work.

Resilient empathy is a relational and equalizing disposition that I insist can be enacted even in a context of racial inequality when we use the Brave Community method. The capacity of the learner or the teacher to extend resilient empathy derives from being previously grounded for learning. In both the moment from Professor Thomas's class and the one from my workshop, there is a powerful sense of relationship, of context, of people knowing where they stand in relation to the content that they are learning and to members of the learning community. That grounding is what allows Cori to do the difficult task of challenging Marjorie with the resilient empathy. That grounding is also what allows me to help Cori, Marjorie, Denva, and everyone else work through the moment. Being grounded for learning makes resilient empathy achievable.

Most importantly, when learners allow one another room to falter and recover, to "say what they want to say," the challenging moments teach learners about their own resilience. Resilient empathy is a choiceful act and legitimate demand in a grounded context. It edifies and empowers the learner who extends it as much as it sustains the one who benefits from it. We do not have to invent often silly or offensive role plays to evoke resilient empathy in learners. We must only create opportunities for resilient empathy to be revealed. In the next chapter, we explore how to do this.

CHAPTER 4

Practice

This chapter shows you how to use the Brave Community method. Although it includes specific activities that you are welcome to use as they are, using them as an inspiration to create your own versions of these activities, customized to your authentic self and context, is better. Before you continue reading this chapter, you should think of a specific situation in which you would lead a group that is learning about racism. If you need ideas for situations, here are a few possibilities:

You are an elementary school teacher, teaching about the violence enacted by Christopher Columbus and others on Indigenous people in the Americas.

You are a high school teacher, teaching about the racial terror of the Jim Crow years.

You are a college professor, teaching about racial disparities in the criminal justice system.

You are a school committee member, speaking about the district's banning of Toni Morrison's *Bluest Eye*.

You are a vice president at a technology startup, addressing the leadership team about persistent staff reports of racial bias.

You are a parent, addressing your longtime neighbors about their "All Lives Matter" lawn sign that they posted after you posted your "Black Lives Matter" sign.

You are a consultant hired by a cultural institution to help the institution develop antiracist practices.

Once you have your scenario in mind, grab whatever you need to record reflections and questions as you read this chapter. Later, you might return to this chapter to support yourself in an actual situation.

PRE-WORK

Grounding Inventory

The *grounding inventory* helps you assess your context before you start your meeting, class, or gathering.

To create a grounding inventory, start with the topic to be addressed, then list the content and culture that you will use to ground the group for learning. In the "content" column, list any text (article, book) or other resource (documentary, video lecture) that contains relevant information, data, evidence you can use to learn about or work on the topic. In the "culture" column, list any norms of engagement, ways of being, and protocols that may already be in place as well as any information that you gather about climate or context. Below (Table 4.1) as a sample is an inventory I used to lead a professional development session on racial disparities in school discipline for an elementary school.

After completing the inventory, ask yourself: "What do we already have in place?" and "What are we missing?" If your inventory shows that you have little to nothing listed for culture, pause to reflect. Is this a case for which there hasn't been specific attention paid to issues of interpersonal culture, but the group gets along, or is this a group in which there is a lot of tension?

Depending on the answer, you should have a certain approach to setting the stage for grounding. If, for example, you know this is a tense space, you may need to spend more time in getting people to discuss how they will approach one another and the learning ahead. If, however, you know that this is a group that gets along well, you may move a bit faster. In the exemplar above, the inventory looks good: There is willingness from leadership, there are at least a few guaranteed engaged participants with some experience (the Equity Team), and the whole group has done some team building earlier.

You must always consider your context. In many cases, unless it is your actual classroom, you won't have a lot of information about the culture of a group or space in advance. In such cases, you should proceed cautiously and assess the context as you go. For me, doing the Backplanning Norms

Table 4.1. Grounding Inventory

Content	Culture
Selections from *Code of Conduct: A Guide to Responsive Discipline* (shared ahead of time).	Staff had a team building retreat in August.
"Glaring Disparities in School Suspension Discipline by Race" article from a reliable news source to be used during the session.	School's Equity Team (five volunteer teachers) attended a training on restorative justice in schools.
School's discipline data (last 3 years) provided by the principal.	Principal is willing to address issues.

activity, which I describe below, provides a lot of information about the context right from the start.

Although you will build up the group's culture as you ground for learning (or as you go along), the content must be there *in advance*. You cannot use the Brave Community method without content. This means that, if your inventory indicates that you do not have any content, you should STOP and go get some. What resource(s) can you use to approach the topic(s) that you are going to discuss? What article, what podcast, what documentary, what evidence or data? Grounding for learning cannot happen without content for learning.

HOW MUCH CONTENT DO I NEED?

To explore this important question, let's take one of our hypothetical prompts from the start of this chapter. You are a consultant hired by a cultural institution to help it to develop antiracist practices.

Brave Community at the Museum

In 2020, several institutions came under scrutiny as part of the nationwide Black Lives Matter uprisings that followed the brutal murder of George Floyd. If you glanced at the news in the United States, you would have read about the latest museum, foundation, or corporation being confronted by its own staff or by the public for being racist or White supremacist. During this period, I worked with a group of museum professionals to develop antiracist practices in their institutions. They were interested in developing antiracist practices for their work. From a Brave Community perspective, I approached this as our learning goal. I would need to ground this group for learning in how a museum is racist and how it can change. This required content that was relevant to that specific learning goal.

I selected a chapter from a book on structural racism in museums as well as a news article that depicted a recent controversy around alleged racist overtones of an exhibit. The content provided enough for us to engage with two essential considerations: the history of racism in the museum context (the book chapter) and a practice-based, contemporary example (the news story).

This grounding for learning allowed the participants to co-construct with me the answer to the question of how their institutions could become antiracist. It also allowed them to place the question in both its historic and contemporary context. We realized that, instead of the content warranting a general discussion about how to become an antiracist institution, or how to dismantle White supremacy, it led us to tackle a critical set of issues with direct implications for their work, in its context. We discussed the relationship between racism and capitalism that underlies the wealth of museums, foundations, and philanthropy generally; how this affects the day-to-day operations of those institutions; and how this relates to ideas about what and whose culture has value. At the end of our work together, the participant with the most seniority told me something that brought home the difference that grounding for learning makes.

> When we started this work, the phrase "structural racism" itself, I am embarrassed to say, felt uncomfortable for me and not entirely clear. I now fully understand what it means and specifically what it means in our field. I also get how everyone's energy that is spent explaining things to old White guys like me would be better spent on positioning new leaders of color, who already get it, in positions that people like me occupy.

Absent the grounding for learning, including the culture that we created and the context-specific content that we used, I doubt that specific and applicable learning would have happened. My role was not, could not be, to tell these leaders in their field how to solve their problems, as I am not in their field or knowledgeable about it. My role was to help them take a grounded approach to their problems, which, as a Brave Community practitioner, I could do.

Finally, then, I can answer how much content is needed. First, the content must allow us to address the learning goal(s); and, second, the content must be bounded; and, third, that boundedness is okay.

The content must allow us to address the learning goal(s). In the example above, the learning goal was to understand how their institutions engaged in racist practices, how this came to be, and what could be done about it. When considering our hypothetical roles, as we did at the start of the chapter, we can imagine different learning goals. For teachers, of course, the learning goal tends to be explicitly to teach a lesson. But for others—the consultant or manager or community leader—we can think of the learning goal as the task at hand, the work to be done The parent who wants to discuss the All Lives Matter sign probably would like to get their neighbors to realize the racist implications of that kind of false equivalency; that is the learning goal. Given that goal, one idea for content could be a short article, podcast, or video about the evidence of police brutality against Black people.

The content has to be bounded. Too many of us feel paralyzed by the belief that we do not know enough about issues of racism to engage with the topic in the first place. We believe that if we do not know everything (an impossibility), we cannot approach the issue at all. I have the most experience meeting educators in K–12 and higher education who feel this way, but I think this happens broadly. As a matter of fact, the content needs to be bounded or limited. The idea is not that we must know all the content "out there" but rather that we have content that serves the focus of the learning. The type of gathering or group also will affect our choice of content. For example, learners in a 15-week semester-long college course will have different expectations of how much content they will be given than will staff in a 2-day professional development or members of an executive board gathered for 90 minutes.

And that boundedness is okay. It is okay because we can continue to grow and learn and do more. Brave Community is a practice. What the boundedness of content does is to invite us to keep inquiring and to ensure that we are grounded every time that we do. In Chapter 5, I explore my own journey of mistake making and learning that it is okay to correct mistakes after the fact. The main reason I wrote this book is because I know that the Brave Community method can be helpful in the context of our very imperfect, human circumstances.

P.S. The Brave Community method is not, itself, the content. This is a nuance that is often missed. Clearly, as evidenced by me talking to you through a book page, the Brave Community method is content. It is knowledge and information that we can use. What I mean is that, when we discuss the foundation of Brave Community, grounding for learning, the method itself cannot be its own content, right? More importantly, using this method does not take the place of educating ourselves and our communities about how racism shapes our lives. Rather, the method, by requiring grounding (and content) encourages that education. I hope that, if you wish that maybe there were more on these pages in the way of explicit direction, book titles, resources, you can reframe that feeling into an invitation to engage in your own inquiry, an invitation to make the method your own.

What about culture? By comparison, determining whether you have the right amount of *culture* for learning in the grounding "recipe" is easier. If you do not have a healthy learning culture established, discomfort and tension will arise. People will be afraid to answer your questions or engage with one another. Learning will stall, and it will be clear that something is missing. Below we discuss ways to boost the learning culture.

Here are some Pre-Work questions to consider, in the order given:

What is your learning goal? When you think of the learning goal for your imagined scenario, what content would you need that would address the goal, be context-specific, while being bounded (because you can't know or cover everything)?

After you have inventoried, reflected on these questions, and planned accordingly, you are ready for Step 1.

STEP 1: GROUNDING FOR LEARNING

Grounding for learning is the foundation of Brave Community, so we start there. Your first task is to establish grounding for learning. By "first task," I mean first *substantive* task after your introduction or greeting. If you have multiple days with a group, it should be the first substantive task on the first day. If you have a few hours, it should happen early in the first hour.

You (the teacher, the leader, the Brave Community practitioner, the protagonist of your own life) set the stage for grounding. How you do it can vary, but the following are non-negotiables:

- You must do it authentically.
- You must connect it explicitly to what learning about racism requires.

You do this through what I call, for lack of a better phrase, your "grounding speech." Before this speech, however, you need to ask yourself: "How authentic do I feel in front of the group?" "How comfortable am I with being authentic with the group?"

Authenticity Is Vulnerability

Grounding for learning requires allowing learners to *really* see you. For me, it happens when I tell learners why doing this work matters to me and why I hope it will matter to them. Something opens up for me when I say these words. I feel implicated and committed, and something clicks. But I can hear you asking: "Good for you, but what if I don't like to be that authentic or vulnerable?" The story below illustrates the importance of authenticity in Brave Community practice.

First Know Thyself (and Thy Context)

I once gave two talks a few months apart at a university in Atlanta. The first was a Brave Community workshop. I was invited to teach the workshop to faculty there in the wake of an open letter by undergraduates, who demanded faculty accountability for various incidents of racial discrimination in their courses and also criticized the lack of engagement with issues of race in said courses. When we wrapped up, the faculty reported feeling inspired and eager to try the Brave Community approach.

The workshop went so well that I was invited back to deliver a lecture to the entire undergraduate college, months later. At the end of that lecture, about 20 or so students of color stayed for the Q&A. They kept me on my toes, sharing a great deal of skepticism about my claims about

resilient empathy and the possibility of productive change. I was particularly pleased that the faculty and administrators present just listened and
let the students have the Q&A. Toward the end of our time, Max, a Black
student, stood at the mic and calmly said that he had "one of those more-
of-a-comment-than-a-question questions." I told Max to "go for it." "I am
just now realizing that *you're the lady* who got my professor so hyped with
your workshop that he went to class the next day and got all in my face in
a really horrible way."

Dear reader, yes and no. Yes, I was "the lady," but no, I had not
intended for any professor to do any such thing. My mouth was dry and
frozen in a smile that tried to hide my panic as Max continued.

> My professor, who is White, just showed up the day after some
> workshop he said he attended, and out of nowhere, he was suddenly,
> like, trying to be extra woke. We were having a discussion, and he
> kept pushing me to be more explicit about what I was saying, and
> as one of only two students of color, I was not into that. He kept
> pushing, and it was so weird, like, that's not him. It got so bad that I
> walked out of class. Yeah, I just want to say, as I sat here listening, I
> just realized, it was *you*.

Max was smiling; he wasn't admonishing me. He was sharing with me
that he now had the much-needed context for what had happened to him.
I thanked Max for sharing. I explained that he was helping me to recognize that I made a major mistake during my faculty workshop two months
prior. I said to Max:

> My mistake was that, in that workshop, I did not stress enough the
> importance of taking time to establish that grounding for learning in
> an authentic way. I did not stress the importance of paying attention
> to your context and how to handle a situation where a professor's
> relationship with students is tense or where these issues have never
> been discussed, and there is no trust there. I didn't spend enough time
> stressing the importance of taking inventory first and then taking
> time to establish grounding in a way that makes sense for your own
> context. So that is the part your professor missed.

Max and the other students nodded, seemingly appreciative of my
honesty, so I felt encouraged. "Honestly, Max, that's just a rookie mistake
on my part. That's my bad. I am still developing this method through moments like this. So I really appreciate you."

Later, as I was packing up to leave, when almost everyone had left the
auditorium, a man I recognized from the faculty workshop a few months

earlier came to say hello. He approached and congratulated me on "another great session." Then he lowered his voice before he continued. "You know, I'm actually the professor that Max was talking about." At this, I raised my eyebrows. "What happened?" I whispered back. He answered:

> Yeah. I mean, I guess, it's exactly how Max put it, unfortunately. I was so inspired and enthusiastic after the workshop that I basically went from 0 to 100 with them. We were discussing Max's presentation, and, you know, there were issues about race that we were ignoring. And I thought I should push us all to be brave. I should model it. But I ended up pushing Max to talk about race more head-on. So I told him it was okay to do that, [but] he didn't want to. He was *very defensive,* and I really pushed, and, I guess, I offended him? Because he just walked out. So I ran out after him. That made it worse.

I felt that I had let everyone down. I told the professor that I was sorry that this happened to Max and to him. I did not have the answers, but I suggested that he write an honest and unqualified apology to Max.

With the benefit of hindsight and more experience, I can say that the professor's approach was inauthentic and did not consider the context. In the absence of better guidance from me about this, the well-meaning professor simply mimicked me in his next class. His students, who never knew him to be comfortable or conversant in discussing racism with them, felt the inauthenticity of the moment. They saw that he was "suddenly, like, trying to be extra woke," and this happened "out of nowhere." Grounding for learning happens with people's involvement—we do it together, and the teacher leads by being authentic. When that happens, the bravery and empathy that come are not sudden or out of nowhere.

This humbling experience taught me to always emphasize that establishing grounding for learning *in an authentic and context-specific way* is essential. In fact, it was after this experience that I developed and began to share the grounding inventory with others.

Authenticity Reflection

An activity to help you get to your authentic teacher self (we all have one, even if we're not officially teachers—trust me) is to answer these prompts in any format you choose:

- What teachers do you remember most and why?
- When you are a learner, what do you need to be successful?

- Engaging with racism is challenging. Why do it?
- Why is your learning goal important to you?
- Why is your learning goal important to your group?
- What are you hopeful might happen for your group? Why?
- What do you fear might happen? Why?

This kind of reflection should provide a rough outline of your grounding speech or activity. Here are some questions to think about: Does the Authenticity Reflection seem like it would work for you? If not, why not? What else might you do to get a sense of your comfort with authenticity and vulnerability for the purposes of your grounding speech or activity?

The Grounding Speech

As we saw in Chapter 1, a grounding speech (or activity) is the combination of moves that a Brave Community practitioner makes to establish the conditions for learning about racism (in that same chapter, you can read about the grounding speeches by Thomas and Stone, as well as my first time grounding a classroom). Those of you who are teachers or who often address groups may feel more ready for the grounding speech. You may already have a style and an approach that feels comfortable. If that is not you, the steps to explore your authentic "teacher self," recommended above, should get you ready to create your version of an academic grounding speech. "Speech" is used loosely used here. As I have described, in my case, it's more of an interactive-activity-and-discussion combination than a speech. I am informal, so I choose to warm up a learning space as quickly as possible. I immediately get everyone involved, and I am explicit about what I am doing and why. As many learners who have worked with me have noted in informal and formal evaluations, I am known to "keep it real." How you do it is up to you, so long as it is done authentically, and you explicitly discuss the challenges in the learning to come.

Backplanning norms is the activity that I use to establish academic grounding. I have used it since my first time teaching, and it was inspired by two things: a crucial interview question from my original study ("When I say discussions of race, what word comes to mind?") and some protocols that are common in project planning.

This activity allows me to begin to build a sense of community right away. It sparks a low-stakes discussion with a new group of learners that allows me to show rather than tell them the kind of constructive community that we can be. When I am fortunate enough to be in-person, I do this after a quicker, introductory activity. As always, consider this script as just a suggestion. As you read, put it in your own voice. Keep asking yourself: "What would I say?" and "How would I say it?"

Backplanning Norms Activity

Ask, "Can folks give me one word that describes previous experiences in conversations about race and racism that did not go well?"

- Write down what learners say (you can use a whiteboard, chalkboard, poster boards, or shared document, or chat if you are meeting virtually).

Discuss words that invite exploration and debate. Some discussions I often have involve questions such as, "What do we mean by judgmental?" "Does the word 'tense' cover it?" "Can you say more about 'one-sided'?" After this first list is completed, shift the discussion. Ask, "Okay, now, in contrast, what are some words that describe ways of being that would best support you in learning about racism productively?"

- Write down what learners say. Again, take the opportunity to discuss and clarify nuance or complexity. Some discussions I often have involve questions such as: "What do you mean by safe?" "Does everyone feel like they can assume best intentions?" "What do you mean by trust?"
- Once the discussion concludes, ask the community to select their top five or so most important terms from the list. These become the community's norms.

Then state:

So, we just constructed our norms. Why did we do this? Because what we are getting ready to do, which is gain greater understanding of racism, as you know, can be challenging for several reasons. To ensure this is productive despite the challenges, we must be intentional. We agreed on how we will approach the content that we will learn as well as one another.

The discussion part of backplanning norms can take as much time as you have, but, ideally, it should at least be 10 minutes. Once the group has co-constructed and discussed norms, they can be referenced throughout your time together. For example, in instances in which you anticipate that things will be particularly challenging, you can gesture to them to re-ground the group if they are displayed in the room (or the chat area of the virtual room).

Questions: When you picture yourself, in your imagined scenario, doing your own version of a grounding speech or activity, what are you saying or doing? How are you accessing your authenticity in your approach? Are you doing an activity like Backplanning Norms or something else?

STEP 2: SUPPORT THE BALANCE OF BRAVERY AND RESILIENT EMPATHY

After your academic speech or activity, a few participants will feel empowered to be brave in terms of how they approach the learning and discussion. Incrementally, as they ask some tough questions or give one another risky answers, and find that nothing awful happens, the group keeps practicing bravery. Although we cannot teach someone to be brave, we can create conditions that best support that quality. The primary way is to ground learners. Once that is done, you can use **bravery boosters** as needed. Things I do often include:

Give people reminders, especially in moments during which I see them becoming hesitant or avoidant: "Didn't we say that we were going to push through discomfort? This is the time to do that."

Give a friendly warning that silence is not a long-term option while also not putting quieter individuals on the defensive: "By the way, this topic is one for which people often are really quiet. Can someone suggest why people might be quiet?" "For my quiet folks, how can we support you to share what you are thinking?"

Help people who are trying to push themselves to stay the course: "You're good; finish your thought." I am careful, however, to never overdo the push. Someone who is about to cry, is extremely angry, or is exceedingly fearful should not be pushed. Instead, that person should be encouraged to take a step back: "Thank you for sharing. I see you are having a strong reaction, so I think you can take a moment. Who wants to pick up from here?" Usually, this allows the group to support the individual who is feeling too much, while also keeping the learning going. It also allows people to see that they set the pace and tone in collaboration with you, that they have autonomy over their experience.

In some situations that do not take place in conventional educational or professional settings, trained facilitators (e.g., therapists, somatic practitioners) may have the expertise to handle emotions beyond the capabilities that I discuss here. The Brave Community method is oriented toward the much larger number of people like me, who do not have such professional expertise. In our case, pushing learners too far emotionally is risky and harmful.

OWNING IT

I have found that it is often useful and productive if I readily admit that I am nervous or apprehensive. Doing this allows me to exorcize my fear: "To be honest, I feel a bit apprehensive right now. This topic is always a difficult one. Does anyone feel this way?" This also opens the possibility to explicitly ask the group to help me feel better, as I am also a part of the group. "I really appreciate the people who are staying engaged in discussion because it is really helpful for me to not be looking at a silent room, you know?"

Resilient Empathy Boosters

As discussed in the previous chapter, as the bravery of the group arises and is sustained, its partner component, resilient empathy, also arises. The initial work of grounding for your learning that you did sets up this dynamic. Once your learners are committed to the productive learning and dialogue that bravery offers, they also become committed to making empathetic space for everyone's bravery. One way to boost resilient empathy is to do so explicitly. As with the bravery booster, you can tell learners explicitly about resilient empathy or highlight when it is happening: "Thank you for saying that. I know that trusting one another right now is a risk, and we all learn from your ability to do that." You can also boost resilient empathy by redirecting the group when it fails to show resilient empathy (as illustrated in Chapter 3). Most often, my implicit way to do it is to set up activities that reconnect learners to being human. Below, I share one that I often use for introductions.

"WARMING INTRODUCTIONS" ACTIVITY

Tell learners that this activity is named intentionally: "Ice breaker sounds pessimistic to me because it assumes there is ice and coldness to overcome. This is about assuming the best and building up our warmth with one another."

You should adjust the directions based on your constraints of group size, context, and time. "As we go around, each person should say their name, the place they call home, and a *favorite childhood memory*."

Alternatively, for a less personal question, if that is more suitable, I say, "As we go around, each person should say their name, the place they call home, and *the last time they felt content.*" I can feel the space, even a virtual one, warm up when people go around and introduce themselves in this way (or do a similar activity). I can feel everyone's gratitude once that happens.

Quick activities such as these remind us of our mundane similarities. They show, rather than tell, how we shape spaces by how we act in them. They bear witness to how we all have favorite memories (which, by my estimation, often pertain to grandparents). The fact is that we all remember the last time we felt content, and we all come from someone, somewhere. This is not all the work to be done, but it is part of it.

As a general rule, I avoid dry introduction routines, such as, "Tell us your name, your role, and why you are here." I prefer activities that are humanizing and surprising. I often adapt protocols from art classes, Upward Bound, and similar programs, as well as popular culture.

STEP 3: MODELING BRAVERY AND ACCOUNTABILITY TO GROUNDING

Blair Teaches Me Something About Resilient Empathy

We are sitting around in a circle because the class, thankfully, is small. Three years into being an assistant professor, I feel like a seasoned Brave Community practitioner. The course I teach our undergraduate preservice teachers runs smoothly and successfully each semester. I even have a good reputation, with the occasional student letting me know at the start, "My friend said I should make sure to take your class because they loved it so much." I am in a particularly great mood because, through a new Honors initiative, I get to teach a smaller group of Honors students. The smaller class size will allow us even more depth. This is only the second meeting, during the first week. As soon as they settle down, I ask students to raise any questions they have about the previous week's class. Through the use of documentary sources, texts, and my own remarks, we established the connection between slavery and the concept of race. Blair raises her hand, and as I turn to face her, she speaks; her tone is startlingly hostile. "One issue I have is that you talked about it as if it didn't exist anywhere else."

I ask Blair to clarify: "What do you mean by 'it'? Race?" I match her agitation with a kind of clueless calm, a tactic known to many teachers in my situation. She responds:

Slavery. There was slavery everywhere, all the time. And there was slavery in Greece. Other places, too. I think to act like that doesn't exist is not truthful. It's not some kind of unique thing that happened here because America is uniquely evil, or something, you know? And, so, I disagree with how you presented that.

Around me, the tension is palpable. Blair's tone is brusque. Her colleagues, sitting in a half circle, facing me, look uncomfortable. Blair is quite passionate and unaware of the million times that I have heard the "there was slavery in Greece" argument. I am thrown off because I felt that we were building community well and did not pick up any negativity last time. I feel offended that she is challenging me out in the open. What I really want to say is, "Just curious how many of your White male professors you challenged lately? Or ever?"

The strength of my reaction lets me know that I am in a powder-keg situation that will my affect my practice and everyone's learning if I do not manage it well. So I ask myself, "Okay, what does the method direct you to do?" The answer is clear, because there are two "go to" moves in Brave Community for a moment such as this, when things go off the rails. Move one: Model the bravery. Move two: Hold the learning community accountable to the grounding.

Move One: Model the Bravery

Modeling bravery does not mean doing the learners' work for them. It just means showing, by example, that vulnerability and honesty, while risky, is not only useful but also necessary for learning about racism to be meaningful. When you model the bravery, you remind everyone that it is possible to do so. There is a first time for everything, but in all my years of Brave Community practice, I have never modeled bravery in a room and not had someone in that room, or even a critical mass of people in the room, meet me where I am.

People often ask me, "How do I know that I am being brave?" The answer is that you feel it. Everyone is different, so let me describe what I feel and where. In my head, I feel a bit confused, not so much that I cannot function but that I need a moment to gather my suddenly foggy thoughts. My mouth gets a bit dry, my hands get cold and I may notice, when I grab something—a pen, my water bottle—that they are visibly shaking. My heart races.

My brain is wired to avoid risks, and answering Blair's challenge was risky, but wholly possible. I knew that Blair's confronting me so early on was scary and tense for everyone. I knew that fear was activated and that fear is not good for learning. I needed to model for the learners how we work through fear. I go for it and ask Blair a question before addressing her substantive comment. It is a genuine question. "Hey, are you okay? Because you sound very upset." She is startled by my question but composes herself and answers quickly: "No, I'm fine." And before I respond, she volunteers a "Thank you," and seems to mean it. "I am okay."

I look away from her and survey the semicircle of faces. They're listening attentively. I see a couple of smiles from students who may feel vindicated by the moment. I make my second restorative move.

Move Two: Hold the Learning Community Accountable

I had started this class as I always do, by establishing our grounding for learning. I used backplanning norms and discussed explicitly why we needed the norms that we cocreated. We discussed how grounding would ensure that the class would be productive. What I said next connected clearly to this.

> Okay, so the reason why I think there must be confusion is that, in this class, if you recall what I told you at the onset, we are grounded in the U.S. context. We are not doing world history, although you should know that the enslavement of millions of Africans was a global event. However, what we are learning is about the particular way it happened in the United States, so we can best understand how it affects society and education here, now. Here, slavery was connected to and justified by a lie about the inferiority of Native and African people, this was that story of race we learned about.

Then, I pushed a bit further, once again modeling that we can be brave and rigorous.

> Slavery *happened* here. It is a historical fact, a devastating one. It has consequences for our lives in this country. That is the focus of this class. So, I think we have to ask ourselves why would it make sense to bring up any other instance of slavery any other place when discussing this country's horrible history of enslavement? That doesn't make sense. What happened here is indeed unique to here. What happened elsewhere does not change what happened here.

Blair seemed to take this in, as did everyone. She had no follow-up questions. The class resumed and went well that day and beyond. Two years later, Dakota, who was also in this class, and volunteered to be interviewed for a study conducted by one of my graduate assistants, chose this moment as indicative of what "stood out" to her from her experiences in my class:

> So I remember we were talking about slavery, and one girl, Blair, she brought up slavery in Greece. I remember immediately thinking,

"Wait, that's not even comparable at all." But the way Dr. de Novais handled it was very admirable to me. She just, she said she had gotten that sort of rebuttal before, and she explained very patiently to them and explained to them why they really aren't comparable. It was like a really eye-opening experience for me that I still remember to this day, because Blair's my friend and she has a really big heart and she's very compassionate, but even the most compassionate people can have those biases. The way Dr. de Novais handled it is the way I want to handle talking about race, even when people don't agree with me. She was patient, very open to reeducating. That was the moment that I realized that I thought this class was going to be very helpful for all of us. It was like the first week of school. Even though the girl was upset, Professor de Novais remained calm, she remained kind, and I think her setting that standard for discussion really helped when it was our turn to have more discussions. Because the way she handled Blair that first week of school kind of set the precedent. If someone said something that another person didn't agree with, I don't think it ever turned heated, it never turned condescending, and no one was really looking down on each other.

The lesson that Blair taught me was that I need bravery and resilient empathy boosters sometimes. As a Brave Community practitioner, you will need them as well during times when a learner or a circumstance tests you. Fortunately, just following the go-to moves can trigger that boost. Once I remembered what my next steps were, I was engaged and curious about how to keep us in the learning.

CHAPTER 5

The Post-Racist Imagination

They want to scare and silence our society back to colorblind submission, where George Floyd and Black people's killability is a natural, everyday feature of American life—unproblematic, unchangeable, and disconnected from the history of anti-Black racism. . . . We need to fight back like our lives depend on it because they do.

—Kimberlé Crenshaw (African American Policy Forum, 2021)

In the Introduction, I said that the Brave Community method cultivates the post-racist imagination. I have not mentioned the post-racist imagination since then. This is because, although the Brave Community method sparks and grows our post-racist imagination, the two exist independently. Like imagination in general, the post-racist imagination comes from multiple sources, and some of them remain a mystery.

I define the post-racist imagination as a mindset, an ability to think through and beyond racism. Because it resides in our minds, our post-racist imagination can grow even while structural racism persists. It combines a capacity to understand racism and to feel empowered to intervene in racism in everyday life—to work to eradicate it from places where we live and work, root it out of our relationships, recognize when it is being used by politicians to sell us something, speak out when it is being allowed to thrive in our children's schools, and so on.

In the Introduction, I spoke of my own lineage, of my being a product of the post-racist imagination of African freedom fighters, such as Amílcar Cabral and others, who fought for the liberation of Cabo Verdeans and Guineans from colonialism. Similar movements swept across the globe between the 1950s and 1970s. Some, like the liberation movement in South Africa, only succeeded as recently as the 1990s. Others, like the liberation of Palestine, continue to this day. Perhaps the most widely recognized embodiment of the post-racist imagination in the modern United States is the ongoing Civil Rights movement. Dr. King's "I've Seen The Mountain Top" speech is the quintessential description of the multigenerational struggle of African Americans for their freedom and dignity as a journey to an *imagined* place that he could see in the distance but might never reach. The most recent iteration of that movement, Black Lives Matter (BLM), is also a feat of the post-racist imagination. BLM is a freedom dream that continues to be practiced; BLM superimposes its dream of Black lives mattering on a reality in which they still do not matter in profound and deadly ways.

This blending of thought and action, this understanding of dream as not just noun but verb, is what historian Robin D.G. Kelley (2022) identified as the lifeblood of the Black radical imagination. In *Freedom Dreams*, Kelley tells of histories that demonstrate the post-racist imagination in Black intellectual and political practice on a global scale. He shows us that Black people in all walks of life create full lives, free lives, inside of a White supremacist nightmare that condemns us to less-than-humanity. This can be witnessed in our past and in our present, in every community that has been racially oppressed. For as long as racism has existed, Black and other racially oppressed peoples have produced thought and action that is fueled by their imagination of a world in which racism does not exist. We have conceived of our dignity and freedom, and made those things real, even if precariously or imperfectly. In this way, Black thinking has been futuristic, and the post-racist imagination has always been around.

The post-racist imagination has many sources, but the Brave Community method is one way to achieve it. For me, cultivating the post-racist imagination is the ultimate benefit; it is the reason that I use the method and am sharing it with you. Without this reason, I would not add myself to the chorus of people already "talking about race" because, if we are not doing it to unlearn racism, endlessly talking about race does us a disservice. The Brave Community method's greatest value is that it sparks and nurtures our capacity to envision and enact a world *beyond* the confines of racism. This chapter is about how this works and why this matters.

ORIGINS OF AN IDEA

I first glimpsed the relationship between the Brave Community method and what I would come to call the post-racist imagination (although I did not call it that then) during my study of Gable University. Over the course of that year of observations and interviews, I observed that students of Thomas and Stone used the learning in their courses to *reframe* contemporary racial issues with added complexity and criticality. The students told me in interviews, and showed through their class discussion comments, that learning about racism helped them to feel empowered and better equipped to confront racism in their own lives. As you recall, this happened between 2014 and 2015, an intense period of racial unrest in the

United States that saw BLM uprisings across cities and college campuses in response to the killings of Michael Brown and Freddie Gray by police. It also included the rise of Donald Trump.

Keli'i described the connection between what he was learning in Thomas's class and his own life in this way in 2015:

> With every reading, sharing of ideas in class, the way I conceptualize my own racial framework, how I deconstruct it for myself, you know? That's changing. The way I see race and how I can see it from different angles, that plays more into my actions on a day-to-day basis.

This connection between learners' developing new insights and their "day to day" considerations of racism's impact was palpable throughout the study. Deyanira, who was in the same class at Gable as Keli'i, described the connection:

> You have a feeling and then you read [the authors in the course], and now when I am discussing with someone, I don't just have to go into my feelings. I can also hand them [the content], the critical work. People always want evidence, right? These classes equip me.

After Gable, I kept seeing this same quality emerge in many learners I taught. This sense that what they learned helped them to better understand the racism happening in their own lives and to discover a capacity, an empowerment in themselves to engage with it. I recognized that this also has been my own experience as a learner: The more I learned about racism, from a young age and then through college and graduate school, the more grounded in my own world I felt. The more I learned about the historical sources and present-day working of racism, the less it felt like some unmovable, shapeless, boundless force, and the more it felt like a system I felt equipped to confront.

Cass, who took my class as a graduate student during the Trump presidency, described how the course gave them a way to engage with racism through "academically rooted" discussions instead of "dissolving":

> I was so insecure entering the course and really felt like I was out of my depth. And I think receiving validation for my comments from Prof. de Novais, I think, really helped me to understand that my scholarly input does not need to negate my emotional connectivity to the subject, like, they can work hand-in-hand with one another. She taught me that I can still engage in these high-level intellectual conversations around highly emotional topics and not dissolve myself

or perform in some sort of way for the sake of learning for other people, that I could stand very strongly in an academically rooted conversation and not falter. I learned that emotions are useful if they activate us, and they sort of push us to move forward rather than get stuck. She created, like, a process for that: In moments when we did get stuck, being able to name why we were stuck gave us a way to move forward and move past it.

Like Deyanira all those years ago at Gable, Cass felt better equipped by the learning that we did in my class. My former undergraduate student Meghan, writing to me during the summer of 2020 protests sparked by the murder of George Floyd, echoed that theme:

> Given all of the recent happenings this past week, the conversations and the protests that are taking place regarding the racism that is ever so present in this country, I deepened my reflection of your course. Thank you for allowing me to have conversations around the idea of race, something that I used to not know how to do. This class has made me think about my place in this world as a White female who works hard, don't get me wrong, but [who] has an undeniable privilege. This class taught me to really connect my understanding, thoughts, opinions, emotions, and knowledge with the world. I feel educated and for that, I thank you.

Whether people call it feeling "educated," "equipped," or "able to not dissolve," what they mean is that learning about racism through the Brave Community method makes them better able to handle it.

Some people reading this may think that there is no way that people's imagination can affect how the "real world" works. There is no way that learners *feeling like they can* begin to make different choices within the constraints of structural racism means much. There are two reasons why this feeling is not productive. One is the historical record I just discussed, the palpable consequence of what Robin D. G. Kelley so aptly named *freedom dreams*. If I am here, a free Black person writing this book in a world where I am neither property nor the colonial subject of White people, it is entirely because people thought it so, then made it so.

The other reason has to do with the relationship between culture and structure, between what we make of the world and what the world is. One of the most compelling explanations of this relationship is critical race theory (CRT). The recent CRT controversy rests on the notion that CRT is a plot to teach White children to view themselves and the United States as racist and, as a consequence, to hate themselves and their country. In fact, what CRT offers is insight that illustrates my point that culture and structure are mutually reinforcing. Created by legal scholars, CRT seeks to address the following paradox at the heart of society: The laws, policies, and institutions are not racist "on paper" (as the Constitution deems that everyone has equal rights, and various amendments, the 1965 Civil Rights Act, and other related policies reinforce this). And yet, we see evidence of racial inequality in every measurable aspect of life in the United States: education, health, employment, and wealth, to name the big ones. In other words, although there are structural guideposts to prevent racism, culturally racist practices have thrived and have baked the racism back into those very structures: The relationship between racist culture and racist structure is a loop. So how do we interrupt the loop?

I need to have a "theory moment" to answer that question. Nothing upsets me more than when people deter us from theory by making us feel like we cannot understand it or, worse, that it is the purview of old White men in high places using exotic words that nobody understands—some of them French or German. That is gaslighting, and you should reject it. Theorizing is a fundamental human capacity. You "do theory" all day, every day, as you orient yourself in your world. You see what is happening on the surface and what's underneath, you think about what someone said out loud and what they meant, you think of what happened today in light of some event from last year. All of that is theory. The fact that some people do it for a living and at a higher level does not mean it differs from what you do. We are homo *sapiens*—the wise ones. Theory, is a part of consciousness, our signature, our birthright.

Earlier, I used the word "reframe" intentionally to describe what learners do when they learn about racism through the Brave Community method. They reframe racism from something that they cannot tackle into something that they can understand, examine, inquire into, and move around. Frames are the way that people make sense of and interpret the world, so they know how to move through it in ways that satisfy their needs. Sociologist Erving Goffman (1974) defined frames as tools for interpreting experience. We can think of frames as a visual metaphor, as the camera and focus button on your phone camera. Frames allow us to understand the world around us by bracketing the action in a particular way (Small et al., 2010). Frames are how we perceive what is happening in this moment, what a situation is really about.

We know from research (and experience) that the frames that our racist society hands us do not put achieving racial justice or equality into view. In fact, they distract us from seeing it. Decades of data collected by social scientists show how people's framing of race and racism—how they think and feel about it—influence how they behave (Bobo et al., 2012). As

I mentioned earlier, we struggle to walk in the shoes of others, especially because we live mostly racially segregated lives. This is combined with the presence of racial stereotypes that can stand in the way of our achieving a common understanding of our racially diverse worlds based on experience and educational curricula that, for the most part, do not address racial justice or equality (Bobo et al., 2012). Although people of color understand the ways that racism shapes everyday life, the majority of White people tend to believe its effect is limited and decreasing (Bobo et al., 2012). All of this creates a lack of empathy across the racial divide. Yet empathy is precisely one of the necessary and powerful antidotes against racism and an essential ingredient for community (Pettigrew & Tropp, 2008).

I want to pause here and clarify that we do not all have the same relationship to these inherited frames. We are not, as some believe, "all racist," by virtue of living in a racist society. Only those who can exert and benefit from racial advantage, which, in the United States, comprises White people and all of the society's institutions that favor whiteness, can be racist. Nevertheless, all of us are confined within, or affected by, the racism that affects the entire culture. So when I say we all inherit racist frames, I mean that, absent some intentionality on our part to throw those frames out, society quietly and subtly slips these inherited frames into place, which make us see what a racist society wants us to see.

When people acquire new knowledge about racism, they get to craft their frame anew. Through learning, people evolve from using handed-down frames that predetermine what they should make of the world to using their self-crafted ones (Emirbayer & Mische, 1998). Things that they could not see about racism now appear clearer, or differently, in this new frame.

Importantly, frames also are future-oriented, as they inform what we will do. For the people whose experiences I shared at the start of this chapter, there was forward motion, not only in their ideas, but also in how they thought these ideas would apply in their lives. To bring us back to our challenge of seeing better in a racist world, reframing how we understand racism involves building your own frame, one that lets you see not only the present world distorted by racism, but also a world that could lie beyond. The concept of frames helps us to see how tightly woven our perspective of the world and our actions in the world are: We need to recognize the world and map it before we know which way we want to go.

When I say that the Brave Community method cultivates the post-racist imagination, what I mean is that it is a way of learning about racism that offers learners a chance to reframe ideas about racism, to make up their own minds after a process of inquiry that is intellectually brave, that goes against the grain. As individuals experience grounding for learning, they are experiencing two things outside of the prevalent racist frames that they inherited: They are learning to deconstruct racism, and they are experiencing that intellectual bravery and interpersonal empathy can exist, even across racial difference. And that experience, that practice, is what feeds the cultivates their post-racist imagination.

I want to be clear that the post-racist imagination has nothing to do with "the post-racial," that bankrupt Obama-era notion that the ascent of one Black man to the presidency and the changing demographics of the nation, with more of its people becoming people of color, would simply undo centuries of racism. Post-racism is also not antiracism, which, although necessary, assumes the permanence of racism. A post-racist imagination is an ability to think through and beyond racism, rather than being merely against it. We need it because, by default, our society cultivates racial ignorance to promote and perpetuate racism.

TWO KINDS OF RACIAL IGNORANCE

Our racist society evolved around the idea put forth to justify violent exploitation of Indigenous and African people, that some people were inferior by virtue of who they were. Today, the idea of an unchanging inferiority in those who are not White is at the heart of White supremacy—the belief that people who are White and their culture are better and more deserving of advantage. This lie is maintained through the creation of a widespread culture of ignorance of racism. This ignorance has two aspects: One is the presence of racist lies, and the other is more nefarious: the cultivation of racial ignorance.

Type 1: Lies

There is a simple, passive "not knowing" that we usually think of as ignorance. This is the version in which, if we imagine people's heads as containers full of information, ignorance is the state in which the containers are missing information. The pursuit of knowledge can be thought of as people filling their containers. Unfortunately, this process is corrupted by the deliberate spreading of lies. When it comes to understanding racism, people are not just missing information. Rather, powerful forces are making sure that the container is full of *misinformation*. Some of these forces are "the culture itself," not the result of individual masterminds plotting (as I discuss below). Centuries of promotion of the lie that some people are inferior and deserving of the brutality of genocide and enslavement produced a whole cultural environment where racist ideas thrive. Sometimes, however, there are people who exploit that environment and deliberately tell lies. The controversy over CRT that I mentioned earlier is an example of this. Below is a brief account of this controversy.

In 2020, his last year in office, Donald Trump stated, by way of an executive order, that antiracist training and workshops were themselves racist. The order denounced these activities as promoting "malign ideology" that was

> rooted in the pernicious and false belief that America is an irredeemably racist and sexist country; that some people, simply on account of their race or sex, are oppressors; and that racial and sexual identities are more important than our common status as human beings and Americans. (Cineas, 2020)

Further, any organizations that engaged in such activities would cease to receive federal funding. Although Trump's executive order was immediately reversed by President Biden in 2021, the ideas in it were adopted by a nationwide, concerted, successful effort by right-wing groups to prevent the teaching of the history and contemporary reality of racism. Under the guise of protecting young people from this so-called indoctrination, community members, school boards, and state legislatures banned the teaching of the history and contemporary reality of racism in many schools. By summer 2022, 16 states had "CRT bans" in place, and many more were scheduled to introduce them. The CRT controversy demonstrates powerfully the exponential speed at which these lies grow. There are only 6 years between Trump's 2015 campaign, when his blatant racist rhetoric was still shocking to large numbers of people, and the reality that the banning of books and firing of teachers for teaching U.S. history accurately has become a common occurrence.

Type 2: Cultivated Racial Ignorance

There is something even more complex and sinister than just the spreading of lies by specific actors. This worse problem is the cultivated racial ignorance that fuels racial inequality at a societal and, in fact, global level. Seen at this scale, there is no longer a set of individuals conspiring in a back room somewhere to spread a lie, as was the case in the CRT controversy, for example. This cultivated ignorance is like the air that we breathe: invisible but everywhere, and most of us do not have the time or the expertise to know where it comes from. When people use words such as "institutional," "structural," and "systemic" before "racism," cultivated ignorance is part of what they are talking about.

The United States does an egregiously poor job of educating its people about the history and contemporary reality of its racism. Germany and South Africa stand in contrast to illustrate my point. Although these nations are in no way free of racial strife (no racially diverse nation with roots in genocide, enslavement, and colonialism is free of racial strife today), Germany has an extensive set of curricula and laws that ensure that its population understands the horrors of Nazism and White supremacy that happened due to their government's role in World War II. In South Africa, at the end of the Apartheid regime, the nationally televised Truth and Reconciliation Commission proceedings brought those guilty of racial violence face to face with their victims to confess and atone. These processes were not sufficient, but they are far better than anything that has happened in the United States to date.

In this absence of an accurate national reckoning about how racism works, the normal human response is to fill our mental containers with ideas that we pick up from people around us, including those in the schools and the media, ideas that may appear to be common sense. In a racist society, however, "common sense" is often racist. As the CRT bans show, although this process always begins with those in power, this cultivation of ignorance quickly becomes the shared project of communities and families.

How does this work? A racist culture promotes narratives that blame people of color for their disadvantage and deny the structured and systematic way that we are disadvantaged.

Consider a popular narrative about Black people: that Black fathers are bad fathers who are not involved in their children's lives. Since this hypothesis was first proposed, scholars have disproven the bad Black father narrative by showing historic circumstances and sociological pressures on Black men and women that have led to challenges in maintaining nuclear families. Black men are disproportionately targeted by the criminal justice system, from a very young age, resulting in many Black fathers being imprisoned by or involved in the criminal justice system in ways that prevent them from building a stable family life. Policies that offer economic support for low-income mothers and children prohibit the presence of unmarried partners in the home. As an increasing number of Black women are unmarried mothers, these policies effectively distance their children from their fathers (Edin & Kefalas, 2005; Mills, 2010). In addition, we know that the fact that many Black fathers are unmarried is often used to conclude they are not present in their children's lives. In fact, recent data from the Centers for Disease Control and Prevention show Black fathers as equally, if not more, likely to be active in their children's lives as White and Latinx fathers (Lopez, 2016, para. 4).

Despite the evidence that disproves this narrative about Black fathers, the narrative thrives in our culture *because* it aligns with racist stereotypes about the inferior character of Black people. It aligns with racist common sense. The pull of that racist common sense is so strong that President Obama himself referenced it when addressing the problems of the Black community. He denounced absentee Black fathers on Father's Day specifically (Obama, 2008). I use President Obama to show that even perspicacious, analytical, well-read, and well-intended people, including Black people, can be vulnerable to racist common sense due to how pervasive it is. The cultivation of racial ignorance is a feature of our system, not a bug; it is pernicious, and it is relentless.

Finally, to think about how the post-racist imagination, cultivated in a Brave Community space, would be helpful against such a powerful foe as this cultivated racial ignorance, let us imagine a young Barack Obama who happens to be one of my students. Let us imagine me, teaching a course on the sociological explanations for racial inequality at Columbia University during Barack's junior year. Barack, who believes that, indeed, something about the character of Black fathers makes them more likely to be absentee than other fathers and that this is the source of much that afflicts the Black community, is frustrated that my class has not focused on this. He is wary of asking me his question because, as a Black man, he feels he would be seen as throwing his community under the bus.

Luckily, we are a few weeks in, and Barack knows, from our first meeting, that this classroom is one in which we encourage exactly the kinds of questions that "raise our blood pressure." He knows that from the Backplanning Norms exercise that we did on the first day and have referenced throughout. He also knows that because he's witnessed his peers do it. In fact, he has participated in receiving some ill-phrased and worse-advised questions from peers with openness and in good faith. He knows that I, the professor, always talk about the need to stay "grounded" in the content of the course. So Barack raises his hand and asks his question.

> Professor, the CDC says 70% of Black men are not married to the mothers of their children. If we keep it real, it's a lot of fathers who have abandoned their responsibilities. You know, acting like boys instead of men. And that affects the families and the whole community.

He takes a breath and closes strong: "We know what the statistics are for kids who grow up with single moms, right? I mean, isn't it better to just be honest about that?"

Because this is my imagined scenario, I am very well prepared and can offer Barack and his classmates an immediate, well-sourced lesson about the research evidence that shows otherwise (as discussed above). I share that data and jokingly tell Barack that both he and I seem to "have done okay, so far, being raised by single moms." I mention that "the data on single-mother households in Scandinavian countries where the social safety net is very strong, and single parents receive a ton of social support, is completely different—those kids do fine." Then I encourage Barack and his peers to discuss the relationship between what the evidence shows us is happening with Black families and what they've been taught to think is happening. "Let's put Barack's question in its grounded context and come back together in 15 minutes to discuss what we think." (End of imaginary scenario.)

The endgame of using the Brave Community method, as described above and throughout this book, is twofold. One, everyone gets a chance to make up their own mind in an informed way. They are allowed to test whether the frame that they are using to look at an issue is letting them see the whole picture or is keeping relevant content out of frame. Being grounded for learning, they can explore this question deeply. They can ask a loaded question, an inconvenient and dangerous one, and find that it has an answer. If they do find, of their own accord, that the frame that they were using is inadequate, they can craft a better one.

Two, everyone is now grounded in learning when it comes to the issue. They are free to conclude diverse things about how the problem can be solved, but to use our example, they are accountable to the content. That content for learning (which again, the Brave Community method would require) suggests that calling out character and personal choices of Black people who have children is not the most accurate way to frame the problem. Why? Because framing it that way directs us away from structural solutions, such as better socioeconomic conditions for Black people or better social safety nets and support networks for single parents, and directs us toward very old (and useless) tropes about the Black family.

The Brave Community method is aimed directly at this cultivated racial ignorance that is the most widespread and insidious because such ignorance has no individual, identifiable culprit. Far be it from me to argue that deliberate misinformation spread by specific people is an easier problem to solve. It is not. But it *is* an easier problem to perceive and call out. By contrast, the automated, cultivated racial ignorance that is the greater, older, thornier problem. It is not a problem that policy alone, without deep cultural change, will ever solve. How do I know that? The historical record proves it.

The bad news is that the Brave Community method is not going to end racism in our time. The good news is that, by leading people to confront racism in everyday life in a grounded way, the method promotes their ability to radically imagine a world beyond racism. It does that by allowing people to have experiences that defy the script of racism; it gives people tools to craft new frames that allow them to focus on the world as it really is and envision, in the distance, the world that could be.

CHAPTER 6

Fumbling Toward Post-Racist Soulcraft

So far, I have shared mostly good news. I have talked at length about the benefits of the Brave Community method and of teaching, learning, and working together to resist racism more generally. I do so confidently because the good news is sourced from research and practice; it's grounded, and you can confirm this by experiencing the method for yourself as soon as you have a chance. I believe in the Brave Community method—love it, really. But it is hard work, and I could never share its benefits without also sharing what it costs. Using the Brave Community method will not always protect us from getting emotionally spent or from being hurt. This is because racism is a scourge that defiles human beings. Thankfully, however, we human beings have ways to restore ourselves. Here is what I learned, so far, about restoration. As always, we start with a story.

PROFESSOR, HOW DO YOU DO IT?

Today's class is difficult. The "Racism in Schools" unit of my undergraduate course in education utilizes Amanda Lewis and John Diamond's (2015) book *Despite the Best Intentions*. The book is a powerful account of how everyday practices in schools in the United States can be discriminatory and sustained by adults of all races, who often feel disconnected from any sense of responsibility. Their rich account of life at a high school reveals how patterns such as the disproportionate disciplining of Black and Latinx students become normalized. As the adults at the school participate in racist practices that they cannot or will not disrupt, Black students learn that they are second-class citizens in their school, as White students learn their privilege.

The reason that this is especially difficult for me to teach about is that my son Jalen and I, like so many Black families, suffered through this everyday racism in schools. For his 4th-grade year, we were lucky that he landed at one school that was almost entirely populated by Black and

Latinx individuals, including teachers and administrators. Apart from that, Jalen was mistreated in school. Numerous teachers assumed that he was incapable or unwilling to learn, or both, because he was introverted and never feigned interest when he felt that certain subjects were not interesting. Jalen asked follow-up questions and sought the larger context for lessons and was thus pegged as being oppositional.

Every year, except for his 4th grade, it was my routine obligation to visit with and repeatedly email his White teachers to inform them, politely, so as not to antagonize them, that their views of Jalen were not accurate. My son was always a model citizen of his school communities and ready to learn, yet I had to advocate, incessantly, for him to be considered worthy of *being taught*. Yes, he is a voracious learner; yes, he is creative; no, he is not being defiant when he refuses to participate once he's already made his point; no, he doesn't think he knows more than you—he simply does not believe that you are superior to him. Because his education was not the practice of freedom, Jalen lost his love for it. This completely compromised the quality of Jalen's life. In my worst moments, it made me a terrible parent who took out my frustration on Jalen. In my best moments, it made me a parent who, try as I might to protect my child, kept sending him into school buildings where he was harmed.

In a fundamental way, every time I address future teachers or any group of educators, the pain of those years, forever unresolved and unforgiven, is just under my skin. How could anyone handle children, those most prized and sacred beings, in racist ways? Even as I teach my students how this happens, so that they may be vigilant and not do it themselves, the "Jalen's Mom" part of me hurts.

In the last 10 or so minutes of this difficult class, Jordan raises his hand. "Professor, can I ask you a personal question?" I tell Jordan to go for it. "Anyone can ask me anything," making sure to look across the whole room with a smile, so they know I mean it. "If it's too personal, I will just tell you that, and not answer." Jordan looks serious.

> I keep wondering, how do you do it, you know, this job. How do you do it? I feel like, if I knew as much as you about racism and all the things you teach us, I mean, I don't know, man . . . I think if I knew as much as you know, I would be super depressed. Or, like, very, very angry, you know? So, my question, I guess, is, "How do you handle that?"

Intellectually, I view this as an excellent opportunity to teach them my favorite thing: how grounding for learning empowers us. Emotionally, I feel tender and vulnerable, and I hope that the students don't notice.

Jordan's question cracks something open in me. There is an intentional intimacy when a Black person asks another Black person certain things in public, especially if what they ask is some form of, "Hey, you okay?" This is even more so the case when we are in a predominantly White space, like this classroom. "Oh wow, thank you for that excellent question, Jordan. It's not too personal, and I appreciate it."

Jordan says a quiet, "You got it," and sits up to listen to me, as does everyone else.

> Well, what's interesting is that knowing a lot about the subject matter gives me confidence and security. It doesn't depress me; it settles and grounds me. Knowing a lot makes me more comfortable taking questions because I have answers. I still feel stuff, but understanding everything as I do, including how we can combat racism, keeps me engaged. This understanding that I am trying to share with you all is what makes us grounded and strong.

Jordan nods and thanks me for the answer. Then class is over. Hours later, on the train home, I am still unsettled. I did not lie, but I told Jordan only half the truth. The other half is what has me unsettled.

ON FEELING LESS HUMAN

I was educated in predominantly White institutions (PWIs) my entire life. Between kindergarten and 3rd grade, in Belgium, I did not know that term, but I did know the feeling of alienation that comes from being immersed in European Whiteness, that intrinsically-superior–acting culture. When I moved to the United States as a teenager, I thought that I was used to it. By the time that I started my career as a professor at a PWI, after having been educated in two elite PWIs, I swore that I was expert in it.

There were two aspects, however, that I did not anticipate. I didn't anticipate how the unbearable weight of my invisibility would be coupled with a conspicuous attention to my Blackness. When you're a Black student in a PWI, you can be immersed in Black student life and embed yourself in that long tradition of culturally specific Black campus spaces. These practices are as old as the presence of Black people in White spaces (or, in my case as a child, European spaces). We have ways of "sitting together in the cafeteria," literally and emotionally, to give ourselves a break from being minoritized everywhere we go (Tatum, 2017). When you are one of a handful in a sea of White faculty, however, the opposite happens: Within your institution, you are such a small slice of the experience that you feel as if you do not exist. At the same time, you stand out as a Black woman who is a professor, precisely because you are often the only one—the only one whom the students have ever been taught by, the only one who studies what you study, the only one whom your White colleagues have worked with.

The second thing that I didn't anticipate was the unbearable weight of Whiteness itself. I did not expect how exhausting teaching about racism in almost-all-White spaces during a time of massive upheaval in the racial politics of the United States would be. My work in schools, communities, and cultural organizations offered some racial diversity in audiences, but my own classrooms did not offer much. At first, the drowning-in-Whiteness feeling would go away once I got into teaching. In my classroom, my students morphed from "majority White" back to wonderful, curious, young *individuals* who were my son Jalen's age and who were eager to learn and change. There were challenging moments, but I processed them. I worked through these moments in dreams, in therapy, in my journal, and in texts and calls to my friends: "Girl, you're not gonna believe what happened to me today!"

But sitting on the train home, with Jordan's question rattling around my mind, I realized that my process had stopped working at some point. Now, I felt deep resentment, deep exhaustion. These emotions, in the context of my relationship to learners, felt like an infection. I felt taken over by something; I felt distorted. This was the unsettled, ugly feeling that I had not shared with Jordan and my students earlier.

When I shared with friends the wear and tear, they'd often say, "You shouldn't have to go through that." Shouldn't I? Shouldn't I be working to get myself and others free from racism? Shouldn't I be supporting the young adults, many preservice teachers headed to classrooms full of kids of color, to become less vulnerable to racist ideology? I should not have to do this work in overwhelmingly White institutions because those should not exist in a multiracial democracy. I should not have to do this work with young adults whose education has given them no grounding in the racist history and reality of their country. I should not have to be the first person to tell them that the category of race was invented to justify slavery and genocide and that, yes, "racist" is an accurate term to describe many policies, structures, practices, and people. I agree that I should not have to do this work under such inauspicious circumstances, but I *absolutely* should be doing it. However, Jordan prompted me to realize that I was not sure how to do my work without feeling less than human.

After the realization prompted by Jordan's question, I went searching for answers from thinkers whose ideas have shaped and guided mine. First, I thought about how political philosopher Danielle Allen teaches that sacrifice is integral to democratic practice. There are individual losses, which we may call *compromises*, that we all take on the way to any democratic collective win (Allen, 2004). Thinking about democracy returned me to Cornel West (2016), of course. West reminds us that an education that is full of "empathy, integrity, and a mature sense of history" (para. 3) is a *soulcraft*. West emphasizes that democracy depends as much on the structure of its institutions and policies as it does on the structure of people's souls.

> For over a century, the best response to Plato's critique of democracy has been John Dewey's claim that precious and fragile democratic experiments must put a premium on democratic statecraft (public accountability, protection of rights and liberties as well as personal responsibility, embedded in a fair rule of law) and, especially, on democratic soulcraft (integrity, empathy, and a mature sense of history). (West, 2016, para. 3)

What West means is that our multiracial democracy requires not just the politics of the public sphere but also democratic practice at the human level, which is what education is about. It requires that we deal with each other. Thinking with Allen and West, I understood that Brave Community is a way to do democratic practice. The missing piece is to engage in the practice without getting so spent, so hurt. I found that last piece, where so much of our wisdom about how to struggle, learn, and change together, resides: in the work of bell hooks (2014).

ENGAGED PEDAGOGY

Critical pedagogy aims to help learners better understand how to liberate themselves and live the best possible lives (Freire, 2018). In her essential text, *Teaching to Transgress*, bell hooks (2014) argued that critical pedagogues must also teach in ways that promote learners' well-being. To practice this engaged pedagogy, teachers must first be well themselves: "That means that teachers must be actively committed to a process of self-actualization that promotes their own well-being if they are to teach in a manner that empowers students" (hooks, 2014, p. 15).

It took me some time to understand that I needed to ground myself in my most human, most authentic self every time I used the Brave Community method. If I did not, I would not be able to restore myself from the impact of suppressing my emotionality—my doubts, my fears, and my frustrations. More importantly, if I did not learn to bring my whole self into my practice, if I did not risk being vulnerable, I could not ask the same of my learners. The invitation to self-reflect that Jordan prompted in me made me see that, in taking care of my learners while not caring for myself, I had been inauthentic and dishonest about my humanity, and in doing so, I had made myself even more vulnerable to despair and alienation. The only way to use the Brave Community method that did not leave me feeling less human was to "learn to enter the classroom 'whole' and not as a 'disembodied spirit'" (hooks, 2014, p. 193). I had to change, and I am still changing.

These days, my *engaged* Brave Community pedagogy makes me give myself permission to be a whole person as I practice. When a learner's comments hurt my feelings, or the subject matter is too difficult, I share that. I do not allow my feelings to clutter anyone's learning, but I take my feelings as seriously as those of learners. This means that I take the time that I need. Time to pause. To drink water. To breathe. Time to collect my thoughts. I tell learners what I am doing when I do it. "Whew, I need a moment because this is hard," I may say.

I also take the time to correct course. Like learners, I make mistakes in the moment, and I cannot always catch and correct them. I now often come back to a classroom, or write a follow-up e-mail after a session, to correct mistakes that I made. I give myself permission to admit the error, even after the fact. "Ideally, I would have handled this better last time, but I was too emotional to do it. So I am doing it now," is something I say more often now.

I pay attention to my own experience as much as that of learners. One example is that, when I am about to teach a subject matter that is unusually difficult, I tell the learners in advance. I might say to a group, "This week is always the hardest of the semester, where students get the most quiet. I hope you all help me out because I feel alone up here." Another example of my growth as an engaged pedagogue is the fact that I no longer do impromptu mini lectures about a topic that I did not come prepared to discuss just because someone asks me about it. For instance, if affirmative action is not part of what we are gathered to discuss or what I have planned to discuss, an unfortunately timed question about it no longer means that I must change course and respond. I have learned to set a boundary transparently with people by telling them that I did not come prepared to discuss the issue that they raised and do not want us to engage it superficially. I may offer to follow up, depending on what is appropriate. It is a way to take care of myself and of them.

In more philosophical terms, I remind myself that Brave Community is a praxis. bell hooks (2014) called praxis "action and reflection upon the world in order to change it" (p. 14). Brave Community is a praxis, a never-ending loop of thinking and doing in service of what I and learners need. It is a work in progress. Because I am someone who chooses to teach people to do this unlearning, I must expose myself to some considerable soul bruising in the process. Drawing from my experiences and the teachings of Allen, West, hooks, and others, I transform the challenges that I inevitably face into sacrificial acts of democratic practice. I turn my challenges into gifts that *I choose* to share and my burdens into responsibilities that *I choose* to shoulder. I have been calling this alchemy *my* post-racist soulcraft.

CHAPTER 7

Conclusion

In 2022, I led a Brave Community workshop to kick off a 5-day conference. My Brave Community presentation occurred as the first event on the first day. As you know by now, I began by using the backplanning norms activity to ground us for learning for the day and the week to come. As always, we ended with time for questions and comments. One of the participants waited until the last minute to speak up. Even through our face masks, I could see that she was nervous. She was seated in the furthest corner of the room, as tucked in as possible.

> I am wondering if you have a sense of how long it usually takes you to know that a group has been, like, grounded for learning? I mean maybe it depends on the group and that's fine, but I was just curious. I'm basically really shy and usually would not be comfortable speaking. To be honest, my heart is beating fast and I am nervous even now. I have been burned so many times where I engage in this kind of discussion as a person of color and then it just backfires, and people don't really show up for it, you know? [I nod; I do know.] So, I'm just curious if you have even a rough idea of how long it takes for it, for the grounding for learning to work, you know?

I ask the participant for her name. Here, I call her "Ana." "Well, Ana, thank you for asking the question, especially if you were nervous! How long did we take to start and construct our norms together?" Ana and the other participants smile at me; they think they know where I am going with the question. She interjects: "Listen, I get it, I think you're amazing, but I just mean, in general, how long would it take one of us, anyone, to do it?"

I stop her and make the joke that is waiting to be made before I answer seriously.

> Yes, I am amazing. [Everyone laughs.] But that has nothing to do with what is happening. It was an hour ago only, right? We talked about our norms and intentions for this week and why we needed

to have the discussion. That is how we grounded our community
for learning. We know what happened and what was said. And here
you are asking a question and admitting you usually would not do
that. You told us, as you were speaking, that you were nervous. And
you admitted that it's because this is vulnerable, that you've been
"burned" many times before in this type of setting, right?

Ana agrees.

Okay, *so I think*, that means it's working. I think you're feeling
grounded, and that is why you feel able to speak up and even admit
to being nervous. I think what we did is what helped you feel like you
should try that. So, it can take that short of a time to work. Now,
don't get me wrong, we need to attend to this, to our community, and
develop our capacity from this moment forward. If, next time, someone
speaks while nervous, or asks a risky question, they are treated poorly
by one of us, then we're nowhere; we're right back outside our Brave
Community bubble. We'd have to recover. But right now, I think, it's
working.

Ana nods slowly. She starts to formulate a question, "But . . ." but
then drops it. "Okay, okay, I get that," she says. For me, her reaction is a
familiar skepticism. What Ana and everyone does not know is that I still
get stuck in that same skepticism every once in a great while. This is when
I become convinced that I have no idea what I am doing, that this method
is not real. Some of it is just my usual imposter syndrome. But I feel that
the voice in my head that goes, "Who do you think you are? You don't
know what you are doing," is also the intrusive voice that gets loud any
time that we dare think outside the box of racism. Because inside racism's
box, we cannot do anything, we cannot find any solutions—nothing we
do works to bring any relief from racist oppression. When that voice gets
loud in my head, I simply tune into what the reality is, like in the moment
with Ana. The reality is that our grounding-for-learning activities done an
hour earlier did help Ana speak up despite her nervousness. The reality is
that Brave Community is a modest, adaptive approach that really works.

Looking back, I realize that I experienced versions of the method as
a student, when I took courses about race and racism that confronted me
and others with difficult histories but, at the same time, left us empowered.
When I studied Charles Thomas's and Isaac Stone's classrooms and heard
from their students, I was finally able to outline the method as a process
that I and others could use. I now practice it and see it working all the time.
Knowing where one is standing and with whom, in a situation where thinking or working on issues of racism will be approached, propels one's capacity

for intellectual courage and empathy. That courage and empathy, in turn, supports learners to feel better "equipped" or "educated" for life in our multiracial, unequal society.

One of the most powerful confirmations of the usefulness of this method comes when I recognize aspects of it in places that, at first glance, do not conjure the ideal classroom, places where I do not expect to see grounding for learning at work. These moments spark both my curiosity and my hopefulness. In 2016, political strategist and commentator Heather McGhee, then-president of Demos, a nonprofit think tank, was live on CSPAN, discussing progressive politics, race, and elections ("Gary from North Carolina," 2016). A man from North Carolina, Gary, called to ask for her help. With the camera live on McGhee's face, Gary identified as White and proceeded to ask McGhee for help with overcoming his racial prejudice. He admitted to fearing and resenting Black people, mainly due to what he saw on the news. He asked McGhee for help in becoming less racist: "How can I be a better American?" In the video, I could clearly see the way McGhee received this question. When Gary discussed his fears of Black men, McGhee, a Black woman, immediately thought of her family, her community, and herself. That woundedness moved across her face. At the same time, McGhee drew from being grounded for this moment. As a policy strategist whose expertise is, in part, the racial polarization of the U.S. electorate, McGhee knew her content. As a seasoned political commentator and public speaker, she also had a handle on the culture of the moment that she is in with Gary. Being thus grounded, McGhee was able to respond to Gary's brave question with resilient empathy.

McGhee thanked Gary for his frankness because it allowed much-needed work to begin. Then she gave Gary some advice by way of teaching him and the public a bit about where racial prejudice comes from and how to combat it. The moment is watchable on the Internet and has been retold by McGhee many times (McGhee, 2020). An aspect of racism as it occurs in everyday life was offered for scrutiny by someone feeling stuck in their racism, and someone grounded enough to feel willing to teach that person that there is another way to be.

In May 2017, Mitch Landrieu, then Mayor of New Orleans, gave a press conference where he took 20 minutes to inform his constituents that he would be ordering the removal of Confederate statues from prominent city landmarks. He combined culture (Landrieu's identity as a White New Orleanian, the norms of a Mayoral press conference) and content (the accurate history of the Confederacy and the aftermath of its defeat in the Civil War, the multicultural history of New Orleans) to ground his audience for learning an accurate version of history. By the end of this speech-lesson, the removal of the statues became the logical conclusion. The speech inspired a book.

On a lighter, but no less powerful, note, comedian Trevor Noah began experimenting with his own version of Brave Community on his *Daily Show*, with segments he calls "Between the Scenes." He allows the audience to ask him questions beyond the scope of the recorded show, and they often ask questions about racism. Noah and the audience are grounded in the sense that they have a preexisting sense of the rules of engagement, the culture of the show, and the "Between the Scenes" format. They have content in Noah's usually well-informed, well-sourced point of view. In his grounded *Daily Show* studio, Noah communicates successfully with an audience of strangers about polarizing topics: police brutality, reparations, the differences and similarities between American and South African racism. Although our problems are not solved when these moments happen, my conviction is that the problem of racism will never be solved without these moments in which racism can begin to be discussed accurately, and unlearned.

When I first conducted my study at Gable, between 2014 and 2015, it was because I was following a perennial question: How does learning about racism in certain conditions influence college students' ideas about racism? Almost immediately after starting my study, however, the United States was plunged into a racist retrenchment that convinced me of the necessity of a method such as Brave Community. In the years since, my sense of urgency has only grown. As I argued earlier, the racist powers that be—here, meant to include everyone and everything that works to preserve our racial hierarchy—are invested in the end of learning about racism for a very clear reason: If we cannot understand how racism came to exist and why, if we cannot examine racism for what it is and how it works today, we cannot envision or work toward its end. Humans progress only after they can make sense of their surroundings. If we cannot make sense, we cannot have agency in our own lives, and we cannot change those lives in the ways that we deem necessary. (If this makes you worry, even beyond the topic of this book, about the relationship between the rampant misinformation that plagues us and the state of the world, it *should*.)

It is not hyperbolic to say that massively powerful sense-making institutions are already captured by a resurgent racist ideology. I have mentioned how, in only 6 years, Trump's openly racist rhetoric became mainstream. There are hundreds of thousands of teachers, students, and communities currently under bans that prevent them from accessing accurate U.S. history in K–12 schools. Higher education is facing the same muzzling, even if some private colleges are a bit less vulnerable. The Supreme Court, one of the nation's most prominent "meaning-makers" on issues of race, has a Conservative supermajority whose Chief Justice does not believe that there needs to be affirmative, proactive action to halt the perpetuation of White supremacy. In fact, he believes that policies that are intentionally focused on racial justice are perpetuating "discrimination on the basis of race."[1] The cultivation of ignorance is being accelerated.

In response, we desperately need to accelerate our post-racist imagination. We need to show how we can meet, as equals, in a grounded confrontation with the more difficult truths about how we ended up where we are and how we conceive of a way forward. We need to experience what it feels like to remove the veil of racist ideology in the presence of others and see ourselves and the world anew. To make these impossible tasks possible, we need to practice. This book is a practice manual.

Notes

Introduction

1. The name of the university where I conducted my study and the names of the study participants, including the professors, have been changed. The names of those whose learning experiences I referenced and the location of these experiences also have been changed. Where needed, details have been changed to protect people's anonymity.

2. Following is an elaboration of these points, supported by some relevant research studies. Learning about and in racial diversity increases our ability to think critically (Antonio et al., 2004; Bowman, 2009; Engberg & Mayhew, 2007; Nelson Laird, 2005; Pascarella et al., 2001). It also helps us to interact with people who are racially different (Chang et al., 2004; Chang & Ledesma, 2012; Engberg & Hurtado, 2011; van Laar et al., 2008) and makes us more civically minded (Bowman, 2011; Castellanos & Cole, 2015; Engberg, 2007; Gurin et al., 2004; Nelson Laird et al., 2005). Scholars who looked specifically at Ethnic Studies courses found that such courses also increase civic engagement (Chapman-Hilliard et al., 2020; Nelson Laird et al., 2005) as well as perspective taking, academic engagement, and students' inclination toward cross-racial interaction (Chang, 2002; Denson & Chang, 2009). Research also connects Ethnic Studies course-taking with a greater awareness of racism (Cole et al., 2011; de Novais & Spencer, 2019; Hogan & Mallott, 2005) and greater cross-racial interaction after college (Bowman et al., 2011; Jayakumar, 2008).

Chapter 2

1. First defined by psychiatrist Chester Pierce, racial microaggressions are subtle acts in everyday life that stereotype or invalidate minoritized people (Rolón-Dow & Bailey, 2021; Solórzano at al., 2000; Sue et al., 2009; Yosso et al., 2009).

Chapter 3

1. I am grateful to my colleague Dr. Jake Fay, who first used this phrase and helped me to clarify the concept early on.

Chapter 7

1. Justice Roberts and the majority of the Supreme Court believe that policies that "overly" attempt to reduce racial discrimination are unconstitutional. Although the legal constitutional argument is complex, in 2017, Justice Roberts

summarized it, using *Parents Involved in Community Schools v. Seattle School District No. 1 and Meredith v. Jefferson County Board of Education*, and stated, "The way to stop discrimination on the basis of race is to stop discriminating on the basis of race."

References

African American Policy Forum. (2021, June 19). *#TruthBeTold: The fight for our lives: The destructiveness of Trump's equity gag order & what Biden must do now*. [Video]. https://www.youtube.com/watch?v=8YxySbIpoT0

Allen, D. S. (2004). *Talking to strangers: Anxieties of citizenship since Brown v. Board of Dducation*. University of Chicago Press.

Antonio, A. L., Chang, M. J., Hakuta, K., Kenny, D. A., Levin, S., & Milem, J. F. (2004). Effects of racial diversity on complex thinking in college students. *Psychological Science, 15*(8), 507–510.

Arao, B., & Clemens, K. (2013). From safe spaces to brave spaces. In E. D. Landreman (Ed.), *The art of effective facilitation: Reflections from social justice educators* (pp. 135–150). Stylus.

Baldwin, J. (2013). *The fire next time*. Vintage.

Bobo, L. D., Charles, C. Z., Krysan, M., & Simmons, A. (2012). The real record on racial attitudes. In P. V. Marsden (Ed.), *Social trends in American life: Findings from the general social survey since 1972* (pp. 38–83). Princeton University Press.

Bowman, N. A. (2009). College diversity courses and cognitive development among students from privileged and marginalized groups. *Journal of Diversity in Higher Education, 2*, 182–194.

Bowman, N. A. (2011). Promoting participation in a diverse democracy: A meta-analysis of college diversity experiences and civic engagement. *Review of Educational Research, 81*, 29–68.

Bowman, N. A., Brandenberger, J. W., Hill, P. L., & Lapsley, D. K. (2011). The long-term effects of college diversity experiences: Well-being and social concerns 13 years after graduation. *Journal of College Student Development, 52*(6), 729–239.

Brown, B. (2017). *Braving the wilderness: The quest for true belonging and the courage to stand alone*. Random House.

Cabral, A. (1974). National liberation and culture. *Transition, 45*, 12–17.

Castellanos, M., & Cole, D. (2015). Disentangling the impact of diversity courses: Examining the influence of diversity course content on students' civic engagement. *Journal of College Student Development, 56*(8), 794–811.

Chang, M. J. (2002). The impact of an undergraduate diversity course requirement on students' racial views and attitudes. *Journal of General Education, 51*, 21–42.

Chang, M. J., Astin. A. W., & Kim, D. (2004). Cross-racial interaction among undergraduates: Some consequences, causes, and patterns. *Research in Higher Education, 45*(5), 529–553.

Chang, M. J., & Ledesma, M. (2012). The diversity rationale. In L. M. Stulberg & S. L. Weinberg (Eds.), *Diversity in American higher education: Toward a more comprehensive approach* (pp. 74–85). Routledge.

Chapman-Hilliard, C., Hunter, E., Adams-Bass, V., Mbilishaka, A., Jones, B., Holmes, E., & Holman, A. C. (2020). Racial identity and historical narratives in the civic engagement of Black emerging adults. *Journal of Diversity in Higher Education, 15*(2), 230–240.

Cineas, F. (2020, September 24). Critical race theory, and Trump's war on it, explained. *Vox.* https://www.vox.com/2020/9/24/21451220/critical-race-theory-diversity-training-trump

Cole, E. R., Case, K. A., Rios, D., & Curtin, N. (2011). Understanding what students bring to the classroom: Moderators of the effects of diversity courses on student attitudes. *Cultural Diversity and Ethnic Minority Psychology, 17*(4), 397–405.

de Novais, J. (2021). Brave Community: Teaching and learning about race in college. *International Journal of Qualitative Studies in Education,* 1–14. https://doi.org/10.1080/09518398.2021.1942302

de Novais, J., & Spencer, G. (2019). Learning race to unlearn racism: The effects of ethnic studies course-taking. *The Journal of Higher Education, 90*(6), 860–883.

Denson, N., & Chang, M. J. (2009). Racial diversity matters: The impact of diversity-related student engagement and institutional context. *American Educational Research Journal, 46,* 322–353.

Desmond, M., & Emirbayer, M. (2009). What is racial domination? *Du Bois Review: Social Science Research on Race, 6*(2), 335–355.

Desmond, M., & Emirbayer, M. (2016). *Race in America.* W.W. Norton.

Edin, K., & Kefalas, M. (2005). What marriage means. In K. Edin & M. Kefalas (Eds.), *Promises I can keep: Why poor women put motherhood before marriage* (pp. 104–137). University of California Press.

Emirbayer, M., & Mische, A. (1998). What is agency? *American Journal of Sociology, 103*(4), 962–1023.

Engberg, M. (2007). Educating the workforce for the 21st century: A cross-disciplinary analysis of the impact of the undergraduate experience on students' development of a pluralistic orientation. *Research in Higher Education, 48*(3), 283–317.

Engberg, M., & Hurtado, S. (2011). Developing pluralistic skills and dispositions in college: Examining racial/ethnic group differences. *The Journal of Higher Education, 82*(4), 416–443.

Engberg, M., & Mayhew, M. (2007). The influence of first-year "success" courses on student learning and democratic outcomes. *Journal of College Student Development, 48*(3), 241–258.

Fields, K. E., & Fields, B. J. (2014). *Racecraft: The soul of inequality in American life.* Verso Trade.

Freire, P. (2018). *Pedagogy of the oppressed* (50th anniversary ed.). Bloomsbury.

Gary from North Carolina talks to Heather McGhee. (2016, August 18). C-SPAN. https://www.c-span.org/video/?c4685742/garry-north-carolina-talks-heather-mcghee

Goffman, E. (1974). *Frame analysis: An essay on the organization of experience.* Harvard University Press.

Gurin, P., Nagda, B. R. A., & Lopez, G. E. (2004). The benefits of diversity in education for democratic citizenship. *Journal of Social Issues, 60*(1), 17–34.

Hochschild, A. R. (2018). *Strangers in their own land: Anger and mourning on the American right.* The New Press.

Hogan, D. E., & Mallott, M. (2005). Changing racial prejudice through diversity education. *Journal of College Student Development, 46*(2), 115–125.

hooks, b. (2014). *Teaching to transgress.* Routledge.

Jayakumar, U. (2008). Can higher education meet the needs of an increasingly diverse and global society? *Harvard Educational Review, 78*(2), 615–651.

Jefferson, T. (1785). *Notes on the state of Virginia.* Documenting the American South (DocSouth). https://docsouth.unc.edu/southlit/jefferson/jefferson.html

Kelley, R.D.G. (2022). *Freedom dreams: The black radical imagination.* Beacon Press.

Kings. (1979). Flor de nos revolução [Song]. On *Faroeste.*

Lewis, A. E., & Diamond, J. B. (2015). *Despite the best intentions: How racial inequality thrives in good schools.* Oxford University Press.

Lopez, G. (2016, June 18). Debunking the most pervasive myth about black fatherhood. *Vox.* https://www.vox.com/2015/6/21/8820537/black-fathers-day

Lorde, A. (1984). The master's tools will never dismantle the master's house. In *Sister outsider: Essays and speeches by Audre Lorde* (pp. 110–113). Crossing Press.

McGhee, H. (2020). *Racism has a cost for everyone* [Video]. TED. https://www.ted.com/talks/heather_c_mcghee_racism_has_a_cost_for_everyone?language=en

Mills, C. (2010) Understanding the effects of child support policy on low-income, noncustodial African American fathers. In R. L. Coles & C. Green (Eds.), *The myth of the missing Black father* (pp. 327–347). Columbia University Press.

Morning, A. (2009). Toward a sociology of racial conceptualization for the 21st century. *Social Forces, 87*(3), 1167–1192.

Naylor, B. (2021, April 30). Biden responds to Sen. Tim Scott. *NPR.* https://www.npr.org/2021/04/30/992355205/biden-in-response-to-tim-scott-says-i-dont-think-the-american-people-are-racist

Nelson Laird, T. F. (2005). College students' experiences with diversity and their effects on academic self-confidence, social agency, and disposition toward critical thinking. *Research in Higher Education, 46*(4), 365–387.

Nelson Laird, T. F., Engberg, M. E., & Hurtado, S. (2005). Modeling accentuation effects: Enrolling in a diversity course and the importance of social action engagement. *The Journal of Higher Education, 76*(4), 448–476.

Nilsen, T. (2019, September 5). Thoughts on the planetary: An interview with Achille Mbembe. *New Frame.* https://www.newframe.com/thoughts-on-the-planetary-an-interview-with-achille-mbembe/

Obama, B. (2008, June 16). Obama's Father's Day remarks. *The New York Times.* https://www.nytimes.com/2008/06/15/us/politics/15text-obama.html

Painter, N. I. (2010). *The history of white people.* W.W. Norton.

Pascarella, E. T., Palmer, B., Moye, M., & Pierson, C. T. (2001). Do diversity experiences influence the development of critical thinking? *Journal of College Student Development, 42*(3), 257–271.

Patel, L. (2016). The irrationality of antiracist empathy. *English Journal, 106*(2), 81–84.

Perry, I. (2022). *South to America: A journey below the Mason-Dixon to understand the soul of a nation*. HarperCollins.

Pettigrew, T. F., & Tropp, L. R. (2008). How does intergroup contact reduce prejudice? Meta-analytic tests of three mediators. *European Journal of Social Psychology, 38*(6), 922–934.

Richeson, J. A., & Shelton, J. N. (2007). Negotiating interracial interactions costs, consequences, and possibilities. *Current Directions in Psychological Science, 16*(6), 316–320.

Rolón-Dow, R., & Bailey, M. J. (2021). Insights on narrative analysis from a study of racial microaggressions and microaffirmations. *American Journal of Qualitative Research, 6*(1), 1–18.

Russakoff, D. (2017, January 25). The only way to fight back is to excel. *The New York Times*. https://www.nytimes.com/2017/01/25/magazine/the-only-way-we-can-fight-back-is-to-excel.html

Schilling, V. (2022, January 22). Georgia school asks 4th graders to write letter to Andrew Jackson on how removal of Cherokee helped U.S. grow and prosper. *Native Point of View*. https://nativeviewpoint.com/georgia-school-asks-4th-graders-to-write-letter-to-andrew-jackson-on-how-removal-of-cherokee-helped-u-s-grow-and-prosper/

Shelton, J. N., & Richeson, J. A. (2006). Ethnic minorities' racial attitudes and contact experiences with white people. *Cultural Diversity and Ethnic Minority Psychology, 12*(1), 149–164.

Singleton, G. E., & Hays, C. (2008). Beginning courageous conversations about race. In M. Pollock (Ed.), *Everyday antiracism: Getting real about race in school* (pp. 18–23). The New Press.

Small, M. L., Harding, D. J., & Lamont, M. (2010). Reconsidering culture and poverty. *The Annals of the American Academy of Political and Social Science, 629*, 6–27.

Solórzano, D., Ceja, M., & Yosso, T. (2000). Critical race theory, racial microaggressions, and campus racial climate: The experiences of African American college students. *Journal of Negro Education, 69*(1/2), 60–73.

Sorensen, N., Nagda, B. A., Gurin, P., & Maxwell, K. E. (2009). Taking a "hands on" approach to diversity in higher education: A critical-dialogic model for effective intergroup interaction. *Analyses of Social Issues and Public Policy, 9*(1), 3–35.

Sue, D. W., Lin, A. I., Torino, G. C., Capodilupo, C. M., & Rivera, D. P. (2009). Racial microaggressions and difficult dialogues on race in the classroom. *Cultural Diversity and Ethnic Minority Psychology, 15*(2), 183–190. https://doi.org/10.1037/a0014191

Taie, S., & Goldring, R. (2020). *Characteristics of public and private elementary and secondary school teachers in the United States: Results from the 2017–18 National Teacher and Principal Survey* (NCES 2020-142). U.S. Department of Education, National Center for Education Statistics. https://nces.ed.gov/pubs2020/2020142.pdf

Tatum, B. D. (1997/2017). *Why are all the Black kids sitting together in the cafeteria? And other conversations about race*. Basic Books.

van Laar, C., Sidanius, J., & Levin, S. (2008). Ethnic-related curricula and inter-group attitudes in college: Movement toward and away from the in-group. *Journal of Applied Social Psychology, 38*(6), 1601–1638.

Vance, J. D. (2016). *Hillbilly elegy: A memoir of a family and culture in crisis.* HarperCollins.

West, C. (2016, November 3). Spiritual blackout in America. *The Boston Globe.* https://www.bostonglobe.com/opinion/2016/11/03/spiritual-blackout -america-election/v7lWSybxux1OPoBg56dgsL/story.html

Yosso, T., Smith, W., Ceja, M., & Solórzano, D. (2009). Critical race theory, racial microaggressions, and campus racial climate for Latina/o undergraduates. *Harvard Educational Review, 79*(4), 659–691.

Index

About the Author

Janine de Novais is a writer, sociologist, and teacher interested in how human liberation is a cultural project—a matter of (un)learning. She has experience researching and teaching in undergraduate, graduate, and professional programs, as well as cultural institutions. She served as associate director of Columbia University's Center for the Core Curriculum from 2006 to 2010. She was born and raised in Cabo Verde.